# Silk Unraveled

experiments in
tearing, fusing,
layering & stitching

## LORNA MOFFAT

Editor in Chief: Linda Chang Teufel

Graphic Designer: Kimberly Koloski

Photographers: Kimberly Koloski (studio),
Barb Schwartz (outdoor)
Lorna Moffat, David Taylor ( personal, travel &
inspiration photos)

Copy editor: Pat Radloff

Library of Congress Control Number 2008924149

Moffat, Lorna

Silk Unraveled:
Experiments in Tearing, Fusing, Layering & Stitching

    1. Quilting

    2. Silk

    3. Sewing

I. Title

ISBN# 978-09641201-0-5

DRAGON THREADS LTD.
*Extraordinary Textile Arts Books*

490 TUCKER DRIVE

WORTHINGTON, OH 43085

www.dragonthreads.com

# Dedication

To David, Cameron and Lily Taylor—you are the loves of my life.

my mum is sewing

# Tearing

### TUFTY PILLOW
## 18

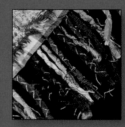

### FRINGED BAG
## 24

### SPIRALS & FLOWERS THROW
## 32

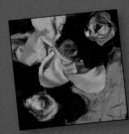

### FLOWERY BAG
## 40

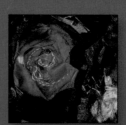

### POPPY PILLOW
## 46

# Fusing

# Layering

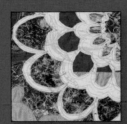

# Appreciation

This book would still be in a sketchbook, with scribbles and swatches stuck to the pages, if it hadn't been for Liz, my mum, coming to the rescue. She spent weeks at a time with us over a six-month period to look after Lily and Cameron while I got my teeth into work.

It was just brilliant to close my studio door and become completely immersed in creative thought without worrying about preparing lunch, changing diapers, etc. Mum, being the sewing magician she is, also helped me construct and finish garments and quilts, saving me precious design time, energy and the mass of hair that I would have pulled out doing it myself. For all this and so, so much more I am eternally grateful.

Special thanks to William, my lovely big brother, and his wife Sandra, my best mate, for the evening we sat with a few bottles of wine, pencil and paper trying to come up with a good title for the book. We had such side splitting laughs, woke up the next morning with no title and headaches all around.

To my dear friend, Sue Pitt, for her words of great wisdom before I embarked on this project. Her ability to shine a very positive light on most things in life is enviable.

I truly appreciate the support from other members of my family and my friends for their positive feedback especially when I went on and on at great length about the projects in the book. Thank you so much for not yawning too much!

To Elizabeth Galley, you were an inspirational teacher and I will always remember how special you made me feel.

Big thanks to Libas Silks for your generosity providing metres and metres of delicious silk to work with— sent all the way to Scotland from California. It was a real treat when the boxes arrived on the doorstep, better than Christmas! Thanks too to my friend, Tomoko Katsumata, who sent a heap of unusual kimono fabrics from Japan.

This book owes a lot to the talents of Linda Teufel and her team (sadly didn't get to meet them, but maybe next time). Thanks to Linda for all her support and for very patiently waiting on us getting our lives together when we came back from Malaysia. It was pretty chaotic because at first we had to move from England to Scotland, and then it took a long time to find my sewing machine amongst the cardboard boxes that filled every room in the house. There was no pressure, just lots of encouragement.

A big thanks to Ed and Inez Smith, neighbors of Linda's, for allowing us to photograph the projects in their lovely Japanese garden!

The most important and special thank you is to my husband, David Taylor, for his love and his belief in me over 26 years together. Without this support I would not be where I am today. Thank you for our two beautiful children.

April 2008

# How I got started

For as long as I can remember, I have been fascinated by fabric. My grandparents owned a draper's shop in the village in Scotland where I was born. When my papa died my mum managed the shop for my nanny Moffat, so my three siblings and I spent our afternoons and every Saturday there. When we weren't colour coding shiny buttons into little boxes, or playing amongst the bags of wool, we were spinning on the carousel for the Simplicity patterns or running around playing ghosts draped in beautiful silk chiffon scarves.

In my house, my mum's cupboard was an Aladdin's cave of knitting and sewing patterns, heaps of fabric, tins of pins, bags of braids, bottles of machine oil and the old Singer sewing machine. Mum gave me access to this special place and from an early age I remember cutting and pinning her old remnants together to make outrageous outfits for my dolls.

I enjoyed art at both primary and high school and in my final year at high school I produced a portfolio to apply to the world famous Glasgow School of Art, built by Scottish architect Charles Rennie Macintosh. To my delight I was accepted.

In my second year I entered the Embroidered and Woven Textiles Department and after five years left with my honours degree, postgraduate diploma and an ambition to set up as a sole trader in textiles. With this training and an idea of what I'd like to make to sell, my textile career began.

My first big commission was for Teachers Whisky in Glasgow. This permanent installation for their conference room was made from leather, silk, cotton and wood, stitched, layered, and cut with areas of the surface painted with car spray paint. The imagery was of the Scottish landscape with shapes and textures representing the distillery architecture and the machinery used to make the whisky. It was hugely satisfying to complete and display the piece and then get paid for it.

Shortly after that in 1988, I moved from Scotland to Canterbury, England with my boyfriend David (now my husband). After graduating from Glasgow University and Durham University,

David was starting his first job with an Engineering Consultancy as an Engineering Geologist. He went to the office, and I stayed at home and worked from our little conservatory.

While David travelled back and forth on overseas work to places like Malaysia, Pakistan, Tajikistan, Laos, Vietnam, China, Turkey, Ghana, Kenya, Zimbabwe and the Philippines, always coming home with interesting stories of the people and places he'd visited, I had begun exhibiting in London and various galleries around England, slowly gathering a client list and working on small private commissions and also working on public art commissions for hospitals, clinics, libraries, etc.

Business really took off when the British Crafts Council asked me if I'd like to exhibit work in New York at a gift fair in the Jacob Javits Centre. They sponsor designers like me to take work to the U.S., subsidized by the Department of Trade and Industry, to help promote small businesses trading overseas. I, of course, jumped at this opportunity and began to create a large collection of pillows, throws and bedspreads. I would take orders from the shows, go home, make the work then post it overseas to my clients. It was hard work! Tons of cardboard boxes, rolls of parcel tape, hundreds of feather pillows and a lot of paperwork—but so much fun.

Over 10 years of exhibiting in both New York and San Francisco, I had collections of work commissioned by Bergdorf's, ABC Carpet and Home, Barney's, Takashimaya, Zona, etc. in New York along with galleries, department stores, and interior designers in California, Georgia, North and South Carolina, Maine, Minnesota and many, many more. This work kept me very busy.

In the middle of all this though I had also moved my work space from home to Highworth Grammar School in Kent. This school, very generously, gave me an office space to work, in exchange for textile and design/craft input in the classrooms. I was their "Artist in Residence". And then when a part time teaching position came up I was offered the job. For six years I loved the teaching, the interaction with the children and working on my designs in a professional environment. Then I got pregnant.

When Cameron, our blonde, bright little button was born, David and I decided to do something a little daring—to "up sticks" and move to Turkey. David wanted to work on a big dam project out there and there was an opportunity for us to go as a family. This was my chance to see and experience a little bit of what David had been doing for ten years on his own.

For two years we lived in a town called Artvin, in the north east of Turkey, close to the Georgian border near the Black Sea coast—in a house made of corrugated tin! We had such a great time, learning the language, meeting many interesting people and traveling around the country seeing the historic sights and visiting the beautiful Turquoise and Mediterranean coasts. I collected many Turkish embroideries, rugs and felts along with painted ceramics and enamelware. I took my trusty Bernina, but with an 18-month-old boy who wanted to paint, draw, dig in the garden, play in the trees, sing, dance and run everywhere, I didn't get much sewing done. But that was okay because our life was very different and our child was very happy.

When this project ended we went back to Scotland and, after a few months we set off again, this time to Sarawak, Malaysia. Eleven months later our lovely Lily was born. David was working on a dam three hours' drive through the jungle from our house in Bintulu so we only saw him at weekends and holidays. This was a challenging time but very rewarding and culturally interesting. Sarawak is a fascinating place. It's one of two states that make up the Malaysian part of Borneo, land of rivers, rainforests and longhouse communities hidden deep in the jungle. It is populated with fascinating people creating art, craft and music.

The Iban tribe, known for their head hunting exploits are also skilled weavers of "Ikat" cloth, and cleverly tooled silverware headdresses. High ranking members of The Kajang have intricately carved wooden tombs depicting the tree of life and the hornbill. The Kayan are the most musical, making the fine, lute-like instrument, the "Sape". The Kenyah tribe construct longhouses decorated with elaborately painted murals depicting the tree of life. And the Penan are also excellent craftsmen in blacksmithing and blowpipe making. The Penan women make exquisite baskets and rattan mats, probably the finest in Borneo.

Our travels were inspirational to say the least. The colours, the climate, the people and their culture made me want to draw, paint and stitch, so that's what I did. In my evenings when the children were in bed, I'd get my books out, lay my fabric on the floor and create. In some of my work I took colours from the wood on the beach, the markings on the shells and the flowers in the bushes. I manipulated the fabrics to create interesting textural surfaces and blankets of pattern.

It was at this point I got a letter from Linda Teufel asking if I'd like to write a book on my techniques with silk. This was too good to refuse.

With two children and lots of travel under my belt, I was so delighted to take on the challenge of doing something different. Over the last 20 years since graduating from art school, as well as taking on private commissions and creating a range of textiles to sell to stores and galleries, I've also enjoyed teaching children, teaching adults, running workshops and getting involved in community based art work. Writing a book is something quite different. I see this as a great opportunity to take what I've learned from my past experiences, simplify and adapt my ideas and pass this information onto others as passionate about fabric, silk fabric especially, as I am.

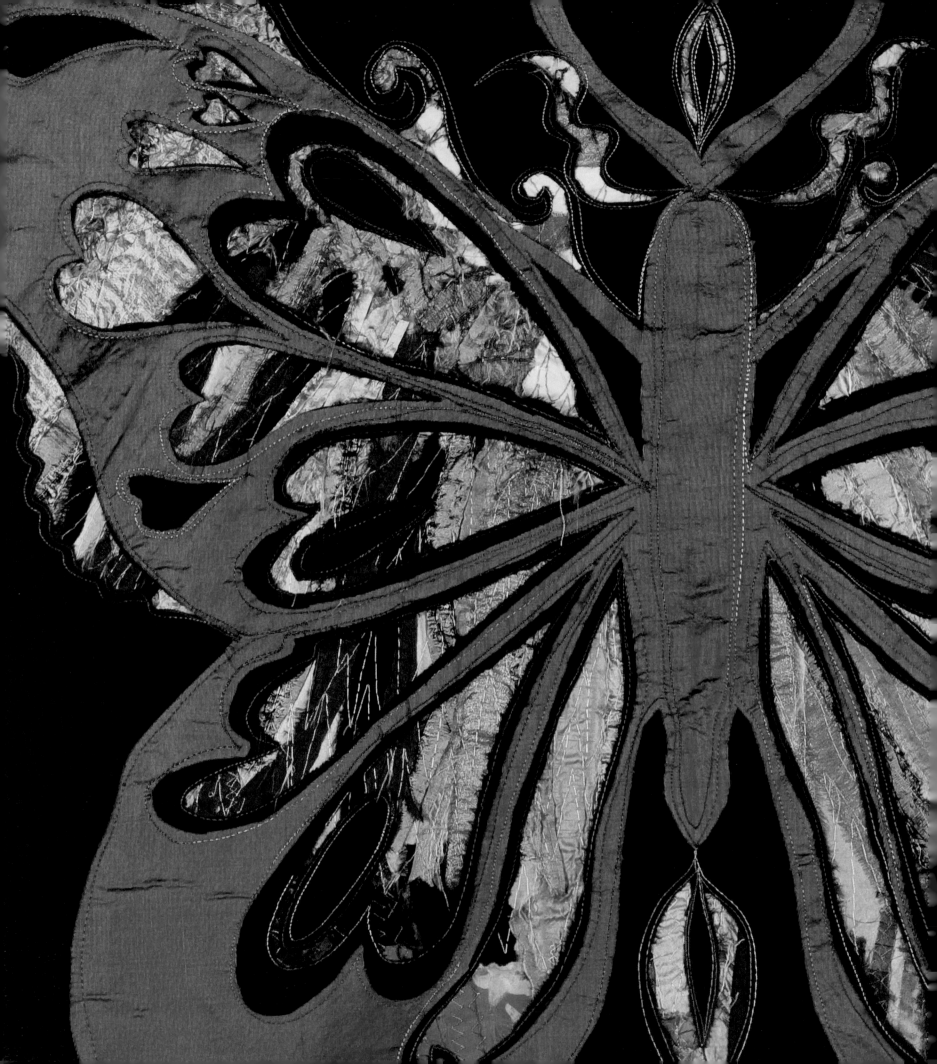

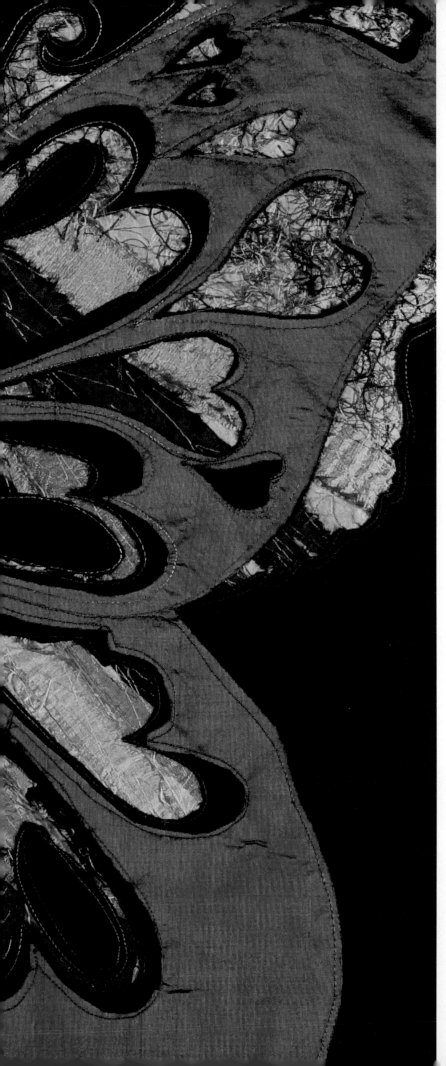

# About the book

This is a project-based book for anyone with a sewing machine, bags of threads, bags of enthusiasm and a desire to work with luscious silk fabric.

Silk is regarded by many as too precious, partly due to its cost, to cut up, let alone experiment with. But it's not until you take the plunge and manipulate a fabric like silk that you fully realise its amazing potential.

There are so many silks, from the finest sheer chiffons to the heavyweight luxurious velvets, each with different properties to explore and exploit.

I've designed 14 step-by-step projects using a variety of silks which include a vest, a coat, a table runner, wall panels, quilts, bags and pillows.

There are three main chapters in the book exploring different techniques; I've called them Tearing, Fusing and Layering. Based on traditional embroidery techniques, they cover deconstructing and reconstructing a fabric, appliqué and reverse appliqué, all with a contemporary twist. The fusing chapter shows examples using a product that I couldn't work without called transfer adhesive, or fusible webbing in the U.S.

This book is about stretching your creative boundaries, exploring new techniques or rediscovering techniques and working with them in a different way. It's also about breaking rules which is always good fun!

Whether you are an established stitcher or a newcomer to the craft I hope the contents of the book inspire, excite, challenge and fuel your creative imagination to develop your own ideas using these techniques.

Personally, the desire to keep experimenting further is always there. Pushing and exploring new ideas is my passion and, hopefully, I engender feelings of joy, optimism and energy in my work.

# Basic tools and materials

## FABRIC

You will have to start collecting a variety of silks in different weights—textures, prints, solids, checks and stripes in dupionis, satins, velvets, organzas, chiffons, taffetas, metallic silk foils, etc. Make sure you have enough variety of colors to provide the inspiration to get you going.

Collect heaps of silk fabric from your stash, snippets of past works of art that are just too pretty to throw away, junk shop finds, silk shirts, skirts that are outdated but when cut up will look fabulous in a bedspread or pillow, out of date swatch books of silks from interior designers. Beg, steal and borrow from friends and family. Mostly I get my silks from the fabric shops. Sales are always worth waiting for, or if there's a fabric I immediately fall in love with, even if I haven't got a project in mind for it, I buy it anyway. I'll enjoy looking at it and feeling it until I'm inspired. Ebay has also proved very useful for picking up unusual vintage cloth now and again. It's worth a look.

## THREAD

I tend to use variegated and solid colored rayon threads in my work. They sparkle and shine and work very well with silk fabric.

For finishing work, such as backing pillows and runners, I use a poly-cotton thread as it's stronger than the rayon.

For some of the projects in the book I've unravelled thread from the bobbins and cut them up to scatter on a bonded/fused surface, or I've scooped up threads from around the sewing machine at the end of the day's work and popped them into a bag for later.

## SCISSORS

You'll need a good pair of dressmaking scissors for general cutting. For the layered/reverse applique work, when you have many layers to cut through, use little straight embroidery scissors with very sharp tips. There are a variety of these little scissors on the market and I believe that you have to try them out and discover what you feel most comfortable with.

To cut the circles in the poppy pillow I used the Olfa circle rotary cutter which cuts perfect circles, relieving me of all the effort of measuring and snipping.

## CHALK

I love my tailor's chalk pencils, in all colors. I can sharpen these to get a very nice point to draw with.

For general marking I also use a big triangular block of chalk.

## DRESSMAKER PINS

I very rarely baste anything together before I stitch it (apart from when it comes to quilting a surface) but I use lots of pins to secure the fabric in place. It's always nice to have a lovely pin cushion to stick them in.

## FUSIBLE WEBBING

It's called many things worldwide but I tend to buy from a supplier in the UK in 10 meter rolls to ensure I don't run out. In the United States, Steam-A-Seam 2 from The Warm Company is comparable. It comes in medium and light weight. Steam-A-Seam 2 double-stick has the pressure sensitive adhesive on both sides which allows for a temporary hold to both the appliqué material and the background material. The appliqué pieces stay in place and are still repositionable until fused with an iron. It comes in widths of 12", 18" and 24".

## CAMERA

I find a digital camera useful to take photos of collections of fabric together, trying them in different color combinations. Then, on the computer screen, I decide which color ways I like best.

## SEWING MACHINE

I love my Bernina. I've used them since art school days and at the moment I have a 1006 and a 801. These are simple machines with 8 to 16 different stitches but I mostly use the straight, zigzag and blanket stitches.

I use the straight stitching foot and my best friend, the darning foot. This foot has to be the cleverest foot invented, allowing me to stitch freehand, draw with the thread and cover an area with stitches like an artist would apply color on canvas.

## REFRESHMENTS

An essential requirement, any time of the day or night, is a good cuppa lady grey tea—my favourite!

BASIC TOOLS AND MATERIALS

# TEARING

S ilk is regarded and described by most of us as special, precious, expensive and something that you maybe daren't cut for fear of "wasting it."

For me, there's nothing more fabulous than entering a shop with walls lined with rolls of silk, jammed up close together—a pulsating barcode of harmonious color, screaming "Buy me, buy me, rip me to shreds and make me into something wonderful!"

It's a joy to take a small pair of scissors and snip along the selvedge of a delicious dupioni, pinch the fabric each side of the cut and, as you pull, listen to the tear. It's therapy for the ears and a good upper body workout to boot.

I think it's important to understand and explore the properties of a fabric before you use it, giving you more of an insight into its possibilities. What I mean is to take a cloth, deconstruct it, rip it and cut it up, then explore different ways of connecting and constructing it— twisting, knotting, weaving, folding and rolling it. These experiments should free your mind of any fears you had about cutting up a "precious" cloth and hopefully provide you with endless ideas for future designs.

Some fabrics behave differently—some stretch and distort as you rip, some curl at the edges and some fray beautifully.

Early on in my career I discovered that ripped dupioni creates a fine feathered edge that, when twisted and caught down by a zigzag stitch, creates little regular tufts which pop out between the stitches.

Short strips of fabric can be stitched in a tight spiral making rosettes which look a bit like blobs of paint on an artist's palette—delicious!

An assortment of strips of varying lengths can be knotted together and cut into tassels and when stitched onto a background, hang like little dancing dolls.

A torn, twisted strip can be stitched to define an area that is appliquéd or cut away, enhancing the finished design and creating a textural and overall more interesting surface.

For visual inspiration look at wrought iron work for complex linear designs, lines in nature, such as ploughed fields, tree bark, ripples in water. Be inspired by bold architectural details, stained glass windows, stone carvings, etc.

In the following chapter I've used these "strip" techniques in five projects—a tufty pillow, a rosette and raggedy petal pillow, two fun fringed bags and a bed panel with a calm green lattice and jewel-like spirals—enjoy.

# Tufty Pillow

**MATERIALS:**

- Patterned silk 24" x 20"
- Red silk 15" x 20"
- Black silk 15" x 24"
- 3 yards of assorted ribbons
- Assorted colors of strips of silk to make 240 tassels for pillow
- Variegated rayon thread
- Poly/cotton thread
- Backing—cut 2 pieces 20" x 20"

This is a pillow you want to run your fingers through!

The thready tassels dance and swing like a kaleidoscopic grass skirt and the colors change and shimmer as they catch the light.

It is a project for the hoarder. To recycle scraps of silk from your basket of bits, tear them up and knot them together. Use dupionis: plain, patterned or plaid, organzas and Thai silks – anything goes.

The tassels are stitched onto a patterned background cloth, the perfect excuse to cut up junk shop finds or the old dress your Aunty gave you.

Bonus! The tufty tassels can be made while lounging in front of the TV, with your feet up and you can get your husband and kids to help, too!

Tufty Pillow

### BACKGROUND

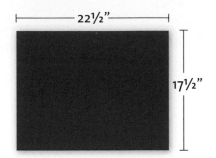

**1** Cut a piece of silk approximately 22½" x 17½".

### COLORED SILK TO STITCH TASSELS ONTO

**2** Cut four bands of red and four bands of black dupioni, each 2" x 22½" long.

Rip as many different colors and weights of silk into 3/8" strips. You will need 30 tufts per row making a total of approximately 240 tassels to complete the pillow.

### MAKING THE TASSELS

**3** Gather three lengths of different colored silk strips in your hand with the ends together. Tie a knot 2½" from the ends and then snip the strips approximately 1" from the knot. Continue knotting and cutting the tassels until you reach the end of the strips then grab another three strips together and repeat as above until you've used up all the strips and have a big juicy heap of little tassels.

### STITCHING TASSELS ONTO THE BANDS

**4** Using a straight stitching foot and a medium stitch length, place a red band under the foot 3/8" from the left edge.

Straight stitch for approximately 1" then place the short end of one of the tassels, at 90° to the band, under the foot with the knot close to the edge of the band. Stitch to secure. Position the next tassel half an inch from the first one and stitch and continue along the length of the band and stop about 1" from the end finishing with a line of straight stitches.

Repeat this for the other seven bands.

Pin in place the first red band, making sure tufts hang off the bottom of the fabric. The untasseled edge of the red band should be approximately 3" from the bottom of the backing fabric.

Set machine to a blanket stitch on stitch length 5 and the widest stitch width. Stitch untasseled edge in position. If using a zigzag along the edges, use anything between a medium to wide width (3 or more).

*Tufty Pillow*

5 Position the first band so the bottom of the red band is 1 3/4" from the bottom of the backing. The second row is layered above the first with the bottom of the tassels just touching the blue ribbon line. Repeat for the other rows.

6 Cut a ribbon (purchased or you could use a twisted strip of silk) in a contrasting color and zigzag stitch the ribbon over the straight stitching line holding the tassels in place using a medium to wide width.

9 To back the pillow see Finishing Chapter, page 126.

7 Pin a black band to the backing leaving a little gap and showing a little of the patterned cloth underneath. The tassels on the black band should hang over the red band.

8 Repeat until all bands are in position noting that the edge of the last band should meet the edge of the top of the backing fabric.

**TUFTY PILLOW**
*Finished Size 21½" x 15½"*

# Fringed Bag

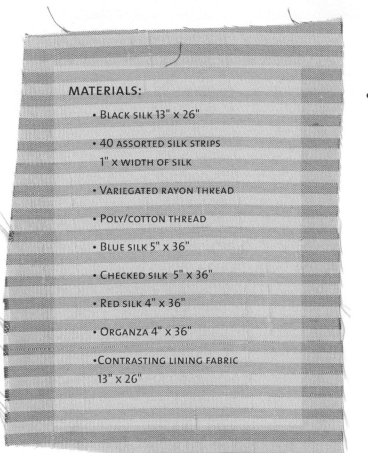

**MATERIALS:**

- Black silk 13" x 26"

- 40 assorted silk strips
  1" x width of silk

- Variegated rayon thread

- Poly/cotton thread

- Blue silk 5" x 36"

- Checked silk 5" x 36"

- Red silk 4" x 36"

- Organza 4" x 36"

- Contrasting lining fabric
  13" x 26"

T his fun, richly textured bag was inspired by the magnificently embellished shirts of the Plains Indians, heavy with buckskin fringes, hawks' feathers and human hair.

My fringes, to make them sound equally interesting, are made from silk that clever little worms have produced and cloth that has been ripped by human hands!

The silk cords of the fringes are made from twisted strips zigzagged with the machine. The top rayon thread and bobbin threads interconnect to form a tight net-like structure around the strip.

Against the dark black silk, the threads are like brushstrokes of color, a dazzling palette which vibrate on the eye creating a vibrant, exciting and original colorful and textural scheme.

### CUTTING OUT THE SHAPE OF THE BAG

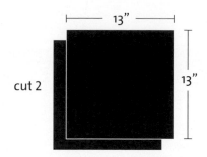

13"

cut 2

13"

**1** Cut two black squares in dupioni 13"x13".

### CHALK MARK POSITION OF STRAPS

**2** Mark fabric with chalk at 3½" and 9½" from the left edge of the squares, top and bottom. These lines will be your guide when stitching on the silk cords.

Chalk a horizontal line parallel to the top edge of each square approximately 1" from the top and also 1½" from the bottom.

### MAKING CORDS FOR THE FRINGES

**3** You will need approximately 40 strips in assorted colors, each measuring ½" x 42" long or however wide the cloth is. Snip the cloth at the selvedge and tear along the grain to make the strips.

**4** Set machine to zigzag and stitch length 3 and maximum stitch width. Roll and twist the strip between your fingers and lay the end of the rolled strip under the presser foot and stitch down the length of the strip. It's interesting to use vibrant colors in the top and bottom threads in the machine.

For a tighter more rigid cord, use a smaller length and narrower width. Experiment with the width and length until you find something you like and make a note of the settings.

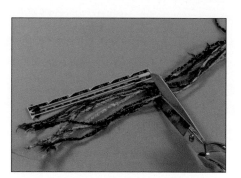

**5** When all the strips have been zigzagged, gather ends together and cut through the bundle at 5½" intervals. You will have a mound of dazzling cords.

### ATTACHING STRIPS TO BLACK SQUARES

**6** Position the first cord at the chalk line at the top of the square.

Center the cords down the vertical chalk line, packing them tightly one below the other and sew them down with a straight stitch. Alternatively pin in position.

Stop at the horizontal chalk line at the bottom of the square. Repeat this along the other three vertical chalk lines on the two black squares.

### MAKING THE HANDLES

**7** The bag has two long straps— one for each side of the piece.

Cut two blue straps and two checked straps 2" x 36".

Iron straps flat and lay the blue on top of the check and straight stitch three sides leaving one short end open.

**8** With a knitting needle push the short stitched end through the tube and out the unstitched end and turn it right side out.

Flatten the tube with your fingers and iron the edges to make the sides of the handle crisp and straight.

### ADDING DETAIL TO THE STRAPS

**9** Strip two red straps, narrower than the main handle and two organza straps, narrower than the red.

Position the red onto the main strap, then the organza strip on top of the red. Pin in place, then blanket stitch the edges of the organza through all layers. Iron flat.

### POSITIONING STRAPS ON BAG FRONTS

**10** Take a strap, an end in each hand and position each end at the bottom edge of the black square and lying in the center of the two columns of fringes and pin in place.

The loop of the strap forms the grip of the handle.

### DECORATING & ATTACHING THE STRAP

**11** Change foot to darning foot with feed dogs down and straight stitch length of 2.

Cut 30 half-inch squares of assorted silks.

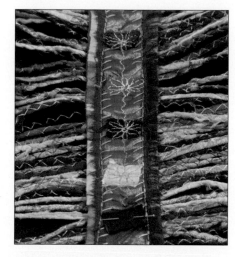

At 1" intervals stitch a tiny daisy pattern over a little square centered on the organza part of the strap. Start 1" from the top edge of the bag and finish ½" from the bottom. Repeat this decoration along the strap and then on the second strap.

### JOINING BAG FRONTS TOGETHER

**13**

Pin handles back onto fringes so they will not be sewn into the lining (see diagram).

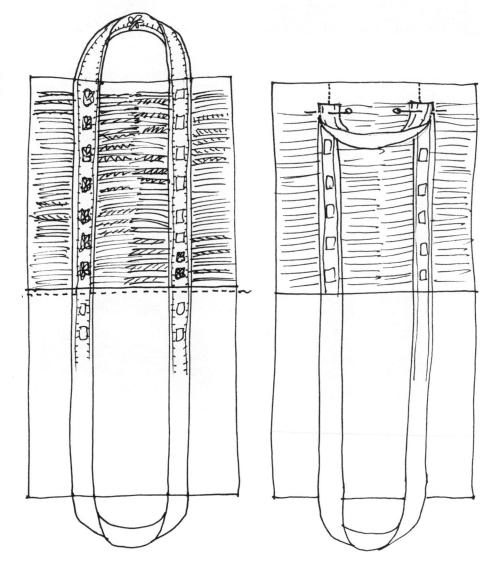

### LINING THE BAG

**14** Cut a piece of contrasting fabric to the exact size of the opened bag—13" x 25" approximately.

Position lining on top of the bag. Pin and straight stitch along only the top edge and bottom edge of bag, approximately half an inch from edge.

**15** Remove pins and turn right sides out. Press with medium hot iron.

With rights sides together, pin down both sides and stitch half an inch from the edge.

Trim and overlock or zigzag edge to neaten up.

Turn right sides out and iron seams flat.

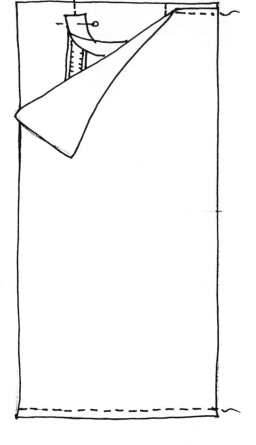

**ALTERNATE VERSION:**

Add a yellow gusset with organza squares and stitching. Photo below shows strap stitched with hearts instead of flowers. Sequins added between straight stitch through center hole.

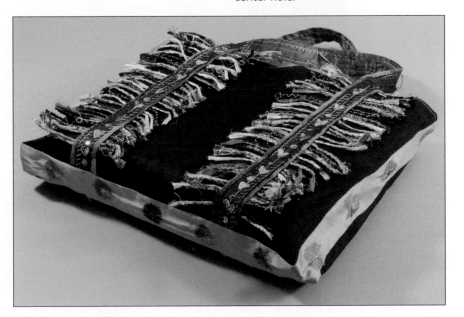

FRINGED BAG
*Finished Size 12" x 12"*

Detail of alternate strap design.

# Spirals & Flowers Throw

**MATERIALS:**

- 60 SQUARES OF 7" IN ASSORTED GREEN SILKS

- 40 STRIPS OF GOLD/CREAM SILK ½" WIDE

- PURPLE SILK 12" X 30" (END BANDS)

- GOLD/YELLOW SILK 30" X 40"

- CERISE 30" X 40"

- VIOLET 30" X 40"

- DEEP PURPLE 30" X 40"

- 30 SQUARES OF 4" SILKS IN VIBRANT CONTRASTING COLORS

- 30 TRANSFER ADHESIVE IN 4" SQUARES

- 60 STRIPS OF 1" X 6" ASSORTED COLORS

- BACKING FABRIC 30" X 81" (MAY BE PIECED)

A decorative throw or panel is an essential interior design accessory these days. It can change the look of a drab cold bedroom interior, add a rich glowing atmosphere and provide a focal point of vibrant, iridescent color.

Nature can provide the most brilliant color of all. Shades of green lend an air of rest and relaxation--deep fir greens, bright pea greens, blue greens, olive shades, forest green, sea green and apple greens.

In the garden, green provides the background for all the eye catching shades of fruit, flowers and foliage. The colors of the spirals and the appliquéd flowers glitter and shine, and are anchored by the green blanket, reflecting the wonder of nature and the magic of the sun.

A throw like this would most certainly get rid of the chill.

I chose not to quilt this piece but a batting could be used if desired.

I have chosen a casual approach when piecing the squares for the background together. Some squares don't match but I like the inaccuracy. Also the lattice lines were stitched on by eye and therefore are a little askew in places, all adding character to the design.

# Spirals & Flowers Throw

### PLANNING THE SPIRAL LAYOUT

1 In your sketchpad, draw a grid of 5 x 12 squares. Then draw diagonals both ways through the boxes. Leave the outside diamonds for the appliquéd flowers and use colored pencils to work out what colors you want to use for the spirals and in what proportions (see diagram).

I've used four different colors, all 40" long – 18 gold strips, 20 cerise, 20 violet and 15 deep purple.

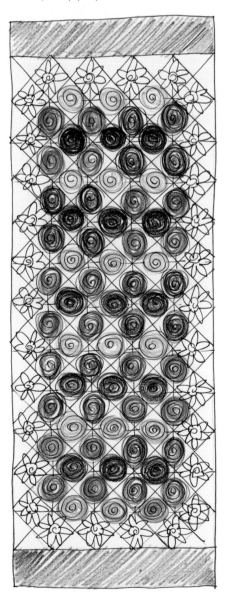

### PREPARING THE PATCHED BACKGROUND

2 Cut 60 squares of assorted greens, patterned, plain or striped, measuring 7"x 7".

Arrange these shades of green randomly together and place five squares wide and 12 squares long.

Join the squares using a straight stitch, feed dogs up and use poly-cotton thread for strength.

### ALTERNATE COLOR SCHEME

This design has a background of blue squares. In the lattice lies a row of florals then a row of alternating cream and gold spirals. This is then repeated to the last row of fused multi colored florals.

With squares together, right sides facing, stitch along the edge taking a half inch seam. Make a strip of 12 squares then repeat to make a further four strips of 12.

Press all seams open.

Join the long strip together pressing as you go so when finished you should have a panel of five squares wide and 12 squares long.

### MAKING THE STRIPS FOR THE LATTICE

3 Gather together pieces of silk in creams, yellows and golds.

Snip the fabric's selvedge at half-inch intervals and tear along the grain to get long thin strips the width of the cloth. You will need approximately 40 assorted strips to complete the lattice.

STITCHING SPIRALS INTO THE LATTICE

4 The lattice of strips should be stitched diagonally across all the squares, starting from the top left corner. Then stitch from the right side so the strips cross each other in the middle of every square and at the points where the squares meet. I do this by eye but you may find chalking the lines to follow works better for you.

Using contrasting thread, the first strip should be positioned in the corner of the top left square and caught down by a few zigzags, then using fingers to roll, twist and stitch in place. Use a maximum stitch width and a medium to maximum stitch length.

At some points in the lattice you will have to join strips together in the middle of the cloth. As you get to the end of a strip, twist the end of the new strip into the end of the first one and zigzag in place. Twisting these strips gives a raised, bumpy line instead of a flat, less interesting one.

5 The gold spirals are positioned in row 2, 6, 10, 14, 18 and 22 of the lattice.

Put feed dogs down and darning foot on and use a medium straight stitch length. Position one end of the strip in the center of the diamond and catch it down with a little spiral of stitches.

6 Then stitch the strip in a clockwise spiral, holding the strip in place with your hands as you stitch. You can also pin in place, then stitch.

At the end of the spiral overlap the end of the strip onto what you've stitched before completing the circle.

For extra strength and decoration, double back over your stitches with another stitching line.

Repeat this with the strips until you've stitched all gold spirals in position.

Fill in the other diamonds with the other colors: 3rd row cerise and violet, 4th row deep purple, 5th row cerise and violet, 6th row gold, 7th row violet and cerise, 8th row deep purple, etc.

Refer to your drawing to keep you correct.

MAKING FLORALS

7 Cut 30 squares of transfer adhesive and iron squares onto a mixture of colored silks in a variety of weights, colors and textures.

On the paper side of the transfer adhesive roughly draw a flower shape with seven or eight petals filling the square. If you don't feel comfortable drawing the flower freehand, then make a stencil. Cut out with sharp scissors.

ATTACHING FLORALS TO BACKGROUND

8 Peel off transfer paper from the flower shapes and position all around the outside edges of the panel, inside the diamonds and overlapping the lattice lines.

Iron over the flowers and fuse in position.

### MAKING THE CENTERS OF THE FLORALS

### MAKING THE BORDER

**9** With feed dogs down and darning foot on, stitch around the outside edge of the shape and then again with a second row of stitching close to the first row. Use a vibrant variegated thread here.

**10** To make the rosette, cut 60 strips of silk, using up any old scraps lying around your workshop. Cut them about 1" wide x 6" long.

Select two contrasting colored strips and lay one on top of the other and position, ends together, in the center of a flower.

Catch the ends down by stitching a little spiral of straight stitches. Working clockwise, twist and turn and fold over the strips in a tight spiral, holding them in place with your fingers as you turn them into position.

As you fold the fabric around, flashes of both strips will be revealed, giving a sort of swirling effect. Double stitch again over what's been stitched to add detail and make it more secure.

**11** To complete the design cut 2 rectangles of purple silk for the ends of the piece approximately 5" x 30" and attach with a ½" seam. Iron seams open.

**SPIRALS & FLOWERS THROW**
*Finished Size 29" x 80"*

# Flowery Bag

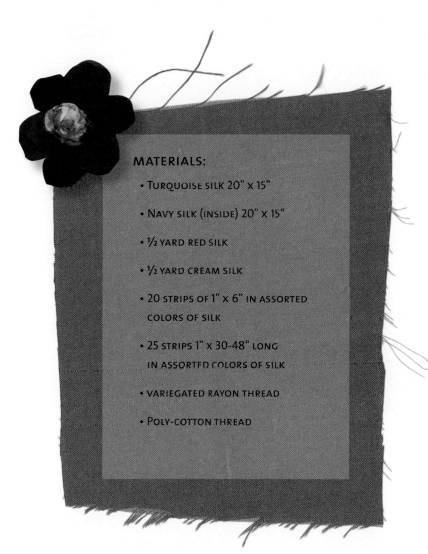

**MATERIALS:**

- TURQUOISE SILK 20" x 15"

- NAVY SILK (INSIDE) 20" x 15"

- ½ YARD RED SILK

- ½ YARD CREAM SILK

- 20 STRIPS OF 1" x 6" IN ASSORTED COLORS OF SILK

- 25 STRIPS 1" x 30-48" LONG IN ASSORTED COLORS OF SILK

- VARIEGATED RAYON THREAD

- POLY-COTTON THREAD

I adore the handle of this bag and it was created in a flash of inspiration. One day I had made hundreds of cords on the machine with twisted and stitched strips in a myriad of colors and I had them lying in a big juicy hairy heap on my desk.

I gathered them up and started coiling them around my arm, twisting, knotting and braiding the enormous clump together.

I realised how lovely they'd be as a long handle to a bag with simply big knots on either end with all their loose thready ends dangling down from the knot.

Simple, colorful. tactile and unique. As for the flowers—well, I'm a girl!

# Flowery Bag

CUTTING THE SHAPE OF THE BAG

DECORATING THE SURFACE OF THE BAG

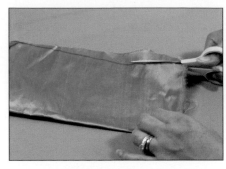

**1** Cut two rectangles 20" x 15" in tur-quoise and navy dupioni.

Fold rectangles in half, then in half again to get a small rectangle 10" x 7".

Measure in 1" from the side at the top of the bag and mark with chalk.

Use a ruler to draw a line from this mark to the corner at the bottom of the bag.

**2** Cut through the layers along this line, curving the corner gently to give the bag its shape.

Repeat this with the navy lining fabric.

**3** Use a darning foot and straight stitch with a contrasting rayon thread on top and stitch flower shapes freehand down one side of the bag from the top to the bottom.

CONSTRUCTING THE BAG AND LINING

**4** Fold fabric with right sides together and stitch down both sideswith poly-cotton thread, following the slight curve at the corners.

Repeat this with the lining fabric.

**5** On the open edge of both bag and lining, fold back half an inch of the fabric to wrong side and iron flat.

Using a 3" length of zigzagged cord, make a loop and pin to side seam of the bag on the wrong side, leaving a 2" loop visible above folded edge. The loops will hold the strap in position later. (make zigzag cord same as in Fringed Bag.)

**6** Place lining inside bag and blanket stitch lining to bag, securing loops at the side, along the folded ironed edge.

Flowery Bag

**7** Make a paper stencil or cut petal shapes freehand.

The large petals are approximately 2½"wide and 2½" in height. The smaller petals are 1½"wide and 2" in height. Each flower has approximately 6-8 petals on each.

I've used seven flowers of varying sizes on the bag and used tones of red silk and tones of cream to contrast nicely with the turquoise of the bag.

Take the petals of similar size and with a hand sewing needle and thread, stitch a big running stitch along the bottom edge of the petals. Overlap each petal at the corners as you stitch, linking them together.

Pull the thread to gather petal together in a circle forming the flower.

Use your fingers to ease the petals into position and use a few more stitches to secure them together.

**8** These rosettes are similar to the centers of the flowers in the Spiral and Flowers panel.

Use two contrasting strips 1"x 6" and stitch in a tight spiral, twisting and folding the strips as you turn to create the blob of two-toned color in the center of each of the flowers.

**9** Pin flowers in position. I've grouped them together around the opening of the bag but you could position them anywhere on the surface. I've also used large and small flowers together. Attach by hand sewing with poly-cotton thread through all layers.

**10** Select a variety of silks in many rich colors.

Rip ½" strips of assorted lengths from 30" long to 48" long. You'll need about 20 strips for the handle.

Zigzag the strips to make the cords, use contrasting threads top and bottom to make the cords really sparkle and leave the threads at the ends, don't be tempted to snip them. The threadier and more raggedy the better.

**11** Lay the stitched cords on a flat surface and gather the ends on one side together and feed them through one of the loops of the bag. Pull them through the loop and tie a big knot in them.

Repeat with the other end of cords through the other loop but this time tie the knot higher up the strips so the ends dangle past the bottom of the bag.

FLOWERY BAG
*Finished Size 11" x 9"*

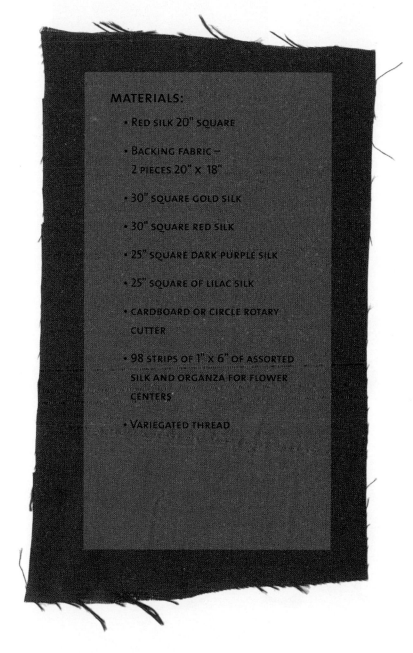

**MATERIALS:**

- RED SILK 20" SQUARE

- BACKING FABRIC —
  2 PIECES 20" x 18"

- 30" SQUARE GOLD SILK

- 30" SQUARE RED SILK

- 25" SQUARE DARK PURPLE SILK

- 25" SQUARE OF LILAC SILK

- CARDBOARD OR CIRCLE ROTARY
  CUTTER

- 98 STRIPS OF 1" x 6" OF ASSORTED
  SILK AND ORGANZA FOR FLOWER
  CENTERS

- VARIEGATED THREAD

# Poppy Pillow

C hildhood memories of tissue paper flower making sparked off the idea behind this design. Circles of color gathered in the middle and squashed together, stuck down with a big dollop of glue—perfect for any Easter bonnet.

It also reminds me of a "prodded" rag rug which creates patterns through the juxtaposition of rags in different colors and textures. It is indeed a very optical, tactile piece.

The purple poppies are the rich, velvety heart of the design framed by the border of flaming gold and reds. The swirling rosette centers of every flower is where the strips come in. They are silk velvet, silk foils, organzas, chiffons and dupionis- exotic colors that sparkle and shine.

Just like taking a sneaky peek inside a magpie's nest, the pillow twinkles!

# Poppy pillow

## Preparing the Background

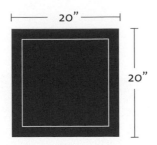

**1** Cut a square of red silk 20" x 20".

Mark a border in chalk 2" from the edge on all four sides. This marks the area in which the flowers will be stitched.

## Making the flowers

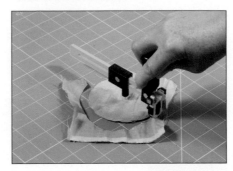

**2** Cut 24 gold, 24 red, 25 dark purple and 25 lilac circles in silk dupioni – all approximately 5 1/2" in diameter. You could make a cardboard stencil for this to cut around if you don't have an Olfa rotary circle cutter.

**3** Snip around the circumference of each circle at about half an inch to 1" distance apart and approximately 1" deep.

Cut 98 strips 6" wide in foils, organzas, dupionis, etc., for the rosette centers.

## Attaching flowers to the background

**4** Refer to plan I've drawn for the layout of colored flowers.

I find it easier if I've got a drawing to work from.

5 Position a red circle on top of a yellow circle.

Place them at the top left corner of the area marked in chalk.

Take 2 strips from your shiny pile which will contrast well with the red and gold and place the ends in the center of the circles.

6 Stitch a little spiral of stitches to catch the strips down, then turn and twist the strips clockwise revealing both colors and straight stitch as you go.

To complete the swirling rosette, overlap the ends on the curve of the rosette and then reverse or back stitch a second or third row to secure. These stitches add to the look and the finish of the blob of color in the middle of the flower.

7 Take another two circles this time with the yellow one on top of the red.

Position them as close as you can get to the previous flower by pushing them together, lifting the edges of the circles up and out from the background cloth.

Hold in place with your fingers and position the next strips for the 2nd rosette then stitch as before.

Repeat this down the left side of the pillow, following the chalk line to keep you straight.

Alternate the red and yellow layers to complete a column of seven flowers.

The second column will start with a red and yellow flower followed by five purples and then a seventh red and yellow.

Complete columns 3, 4, 5 and 6 as above with final 7th – a row of reds and gold to complete.

8 To back the pillow see Finishing Chapter, page 126.

**POPPY PILLOW**
*Finished Size 16" x 16"*

# Texture

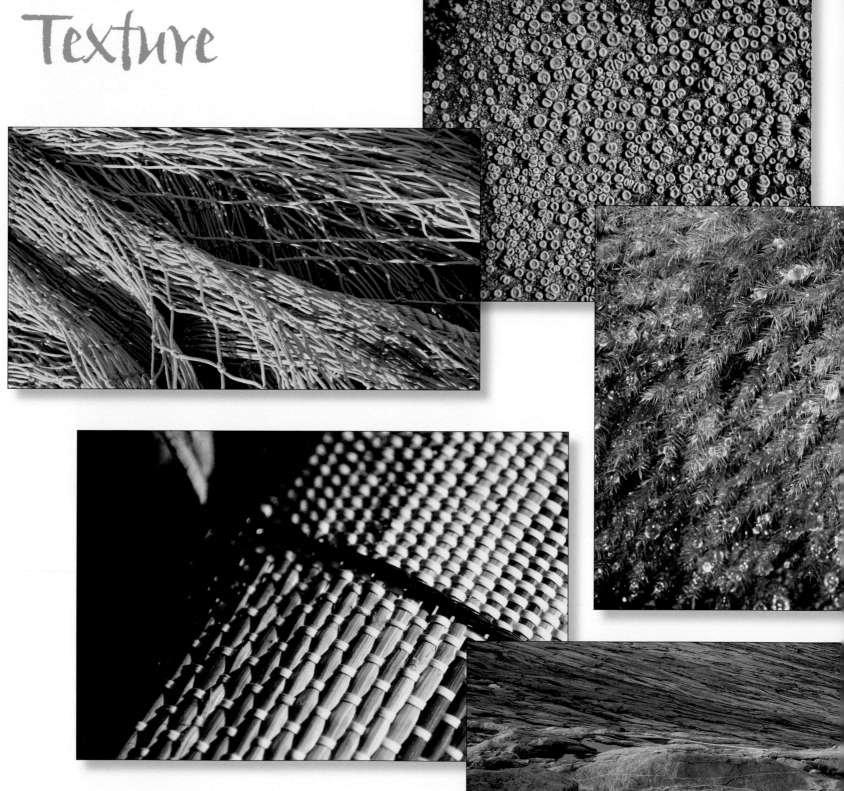

53

# Architecture

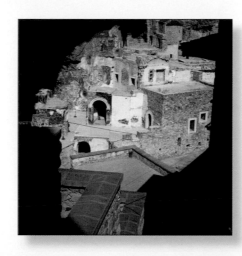

INSPIRATION

# FUSING

**T**his is about one of the most versatile products available to us in the textile world – it goes by a variety of names, so you might recognize it as Bond-a-web, or transfer adhesive, or Steam-A-Seam 2 in the U.S.

I love it! It is fusible webbing and is readily available by the yard in most craft shops and sewing supply stores.

Steam-A-Seam 2 is a fusible webbing that has adhesive on both sides under paper backing. It fuses fabrics together simply by ironing. It can be used for appliqué, trapping or layering of fabric and collage. I have used it mainly for appliqué and collage and only occasionally for putting up hems! It comes in regular or light weight.

On many occasions it has proved invaluable when working on large scale panels. The adhesive coated webbing is great for holding everything in place before you take it to the sewing machine.

Fabulous textural surfaces can be invented just by using snippets of cloth or threads scattered onto the adhesive side. In this chapter I've shown some examples of how you can create such fabrics. It's also a great way to use the threads you sweep up off the floor – stitch it, don't ditch it!!

As I've already mentioned, there's paper on one side of this product which means you can draw on it, and if you can't draw—simply trace. Once you've ironed the transfer adhesive onto the silk you can draw designs on the paper, then cut your shape out very accurately and with crisp sharp lines. Alternatively, you can trace a motif or design from a book onto the paper side, iron onto a fabric, then cut—it's easy!

In the Crystal pillow and Eternity quilt projects I was inspired to create my designs when I researched the use of paper and its rich history in folk art. Cut paper designs have been decorating Polish interiors since the early nineteenth century and they reflect a particularly high level of artistry. I think that this technique lends itself to fused fabric so well.

I fashioned the designs for the trees, leaves, fruits and big crystal from folded and cut fused silk. I drew my designs on the folded paper side of the fabric, then very carefully cut out the shapes. I discovered that I could create something that looks very intricate and complicated with very simple lines and accurate cutting.

**I**n the cut curtain project I've created a lacy structure with two contrasting sides, that work in harmony together. The fusing between the layers not only sticks them together but it gives the panel strength and body and the glue glistens through the chiffon.

The tile style pillow project is pure appliqué—accurately cut shapes fused on to a background, stitched and layered together—simple, colorful and lots of fun.

Using this amazing product along with the sewing machine we, as designers, can rise to the challenge of huge scale commissions with confidence when we have transfer adhesive holding everything in place before stitching. We can create images which are bold, crisp, graphic and precise. We can also create a unique textural surface by scattering confetti-like pieces of glossy threads and fabrics onto a surface that will make viewers want to sink into its den of colors.

# Tile Style Pillow

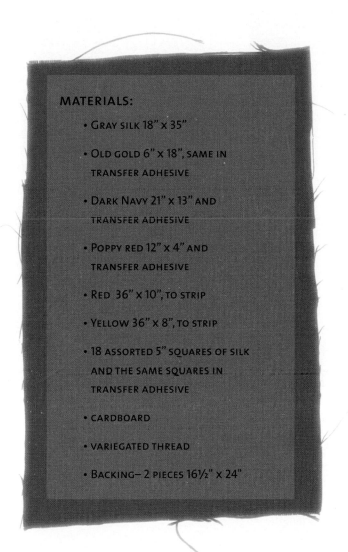

**MATERIALS:**

- GRAY SILK 18" x 35"

- OLD GOLD 6" x 18", SAME IN TRANSFER ADHESIVE

- DARK NAVY 21" x 13" AND TRANSFER ADHESIVE

- POPPY RED 12" x 4" AND TRANSFER ADHESIVE

- RED 36" x 10", TO STRIP

- YELLOW 36" x 8", TO STRIP

- 18 ASSORTED 5" SQUARES OF SILK AND THE SAME SQUARES IN TRANSFER ADHESIVE

- CARDBOARD

- VARIEGATED THREAD

- BACKING— 2 PIECES 16½" x 24"

A s I mentioned in the introduction to this chapter, this project is about appliqué and layering one shape over another, assisted by our trusty transfer adhesive.

In contrast with the previous pillows, this is more graphic and has a lovely smooth surface. When the pillow is stuffed it takes its shape and the colors shine beautifully, changing in different lights.

Taking a very simple pattern or shape and repeating it over a surface can be incredibly effective and it's so much more interesting if you play with changing the color or the position of the shapes within the composition.

The stone gray background is a perfect anchor color for all the vibrant, pigeonhole-like squares of silk. And I had a lot of fun playing with the positioning of the hearts, which have ended up facing one another. They could be birds in their spiky nests having a nose in each other's colorful space.

I have also used my favorite technique strips of silks zig-zagged over the squares just to give the surface a few thready bumps on the pillow's smooth surface.

# Tile Style Pillow

## CUTTING THE FABRIC & ADHESIVE

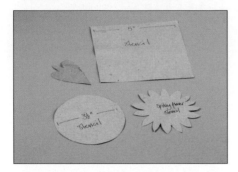

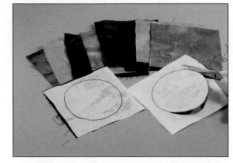

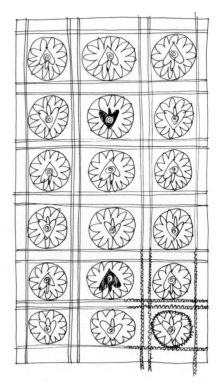

**1** Make cardboard templates of a 3½" circle, a heart shape, a spiky flower and a 5" square.

Measure and cut a rectangular piece of gray silk 18"x 34½ .

Cut an antique gold colored silk 6"x 18" and the same in transfer adhesive.

Cut a dark navy silk 21"x 13" and the same in transfer adhesive.

Cut a poppy red silk, 12"x 4" and the same in transfer adhesive.

**2** Cut 18 squares, 5"x 5" of jewel colored dupionis and the same in transfer adhesive.

Using a medium hot iron, fuse the transfer adhesive to the 18 squares, placing glue side down and paper side facing up.

Take the cardboard stencil of a circle 3½" in diameter and draw around it in the middle of each of the paper-backed fused squares. Cut out the circles.

## ARRANGING & FUSING COLORED SQUARES

**3** Fuse the transfer adhesive to the navy silk and, using the template as a guide, trace and then cut out 16 spiky petalled flowers making sure they're no larger than the circle. Also draw and cut out two navy heart shapes, using stencils.

Fuse transfer adhesive to the red silk and cut out two spiky flowers.

Fuse transfer adhesive to the old gold silk and draw and cut out 16 heart shapes.

**4** Position three squares along the width and six down the length of the gray silk. Leave a 1" border on all four sides and a half inch space between each square. When you have decided on the layout of colors, peel off the paper backing, position on gray and fuse, using a medium hot iron.

## MAKE STRIPS TO FRAME THE SQUARES

**5** Select red and golden yellow silk to snip and tear to create long strips.

Make the following:

4 strips of red and 2 of yellow 1"x 35"

6 strips of red and 6 of yellow 1"x 18"

### STITCHING THE STRIPS

6 The long yellow strips are twisted and zigzagged into position along the edge of the squares down the 1st row of 6 squares and the 3rd row of 6. The long red strips are stitched down the middle row of 6.

The short yellow strips are zigzagged across the 1st, 3rd and 5th rows of 3 squares and the short reds across the squares in the 2nd, 4th and 6th rows.

### STITCHING THE EDGE OF THE CIRCLES

7 Use multicolored rayon threads to stitch a tight and wide zigzag around the edge of all the circles.

### FUSING THE FLOWERS.

8 Peel off the paper and position flowers in the center of the circles, placing a red flower in the middle square of row 2 and 5.

### STITCHING THE FLOWERS

9 Using a darning foot, straight stitch around the edge of the spiky petals. Stitch around the shape twice.

### FUSING AND STITCHING THE HEARTS

10 Peel off paper backing and position the hearts in the center of the flowers and stitch in place using a tight, narrow zigzag.

### DETAIL IN THE CENTERS OF THE HEARTS

11 Cut out 18 small circles of multi-colored silks, pin in the middle of each heart and stitch a spiral of straight stitches in a contrasting thread to complete the design.

For pillow backing see Finishing chapter, page 126.

Add a little flower to the smaller panel on the back for a little added detail.

**TILE STYLE PILLOW**
*Finished Size 15½" x 31½"*

# Crystal Pillow

**MATERIALS:**

- Dark blue dupioni 20" square

- Vanilla dupioni 20" square

- Transfer adhesive 40" x 20"

- Lots of assorted silks 1" wide and varying lengths in many colors – approximately 10 yards long when stitched end to end

- Acid green silk or chiffon for spiral detail

- Backing fabric– two pieces 20" x 18"

- Variegated thread

A brilliant bold motif lies confidently on top of a mesmerizing whirlpool of watery blues, greens and reds. It's a giant snowflake that's never going to melt. The fluid lines draw us in and keep our eyes busy. I have used familiar color combinations that have fresh, vitalizing qualities and overall are invigorating. They are "cool" but not cold.

There's an interesting combination of a highly textural background and contrasting smooth, crisp symbol in the foreground.

The long multi-colored ribbon of strips for the pillow's background was made of scraps of silk from old boxes of remnants, some of which I hadn't seen for a long time, so it was like finding old friends in there. I remembered what I had made with them and who I made them for and when. The spiraling ribbon of color is my pool of memories.

# Crystal Pillow

### PREPARING BACKGROUND FABRIC

1 Cut dark blue dupioni 20" x 20"

Cut transfer adhesive 20" x 20"

Place transfer adhesive, paper side up, on top of the blue silk and fuse with a medium hot iron.

Carefully peel off the paper and save it for later steps. Leave to one side.

### MAKING STRIPS FOR BACKGROUND SPIRAL

2 Tear 1" strips of lots of different colors of dupioni, organza, taffeta—whatever's in your box of scraps. Cut them anywhere between 6"- 10" long. These strips will be stitched end to end to make a long ribbon of strips approximately 10 yards long to create the spiral.

### STITCHING STRIPS TOGETHER

3 With a straight stitch, join the strips together, placing them end to end and overlapping them by about 1 to 2" as you go. Option: use a variegated thread.

Mix the colors and textures of the strips so you finish up with a lovely long, multicolored ribbon.

### FUSING RIBBON TO THE BACKGROUND

4 Position or pin one end of the long ribbon in the center of the blue square.

Lay the ribbon in a spiral, moving in a clockwise direction from the center. Twist and fold the strips where necessary and pin as you go until you reach the edges of the silk square.

5 Fill in the four corners of the square with shorter lengths of the ribbon, getting shorter as you reach the corner points.

Use the paper you peeled off the transfer adhesive earlier and lay carefully over the spiralling strips.

Iron and fuse into position.

Remember to remove all the pins once fusing is complete.

### STITCHING RIBBON INTO POSITION

6 Stitch using a big zigzag stitch with feed dogs up and variegated rayon thread to compliment the colors in the strips.

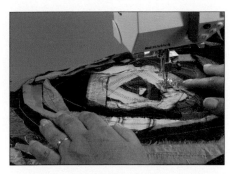

**7** Start in the center of the square and stitch over the strips, following the twists and curves of the spiral until you get to the edge of the square. Stitch over all the strips at the corners in the same way.

This is enough to catch the strips and hold them down but, if you want, you could go over the spiral several times with straight stitch or with more zigzags for added stability.

**8** For added texture and detail I have used green chiffon which I have ripped into strips. Then I've zigzagged these green strips in place, between the ribbon's spiral, thus creating a spiral within a spiral.

### THE CRYSTAL OVERLAY

**9** Cut a vanilla silk 18" x 18".

Cut transfer adhesive 18" x 18".

Fuse transfer adhesive to the silk square.

Fold the fused fabric in half then half again and draw, using a pencil, a quarter of the circular crystal motif (see pattern on page 130).

You could use a compass to get a very accurate circular shape and then draw within the circle or you can, like me, do it by eye so it's not quite a perfect circular shape when you unfold the fabric.

**10** Use small, sharp scissors and cut through all layers following your drawing lines.

### FUSING CRYSTAL TO BACKGROUND

**11** Peel paper off crystal motif and lay it in the center of the background, glue side down, and leave a 1" space around all 4 sides. Fuse using a medium hot iron.

### STITCHING THE MOTIF IN POSITION

**12** Use straight stitch, with darning foot and feed dogs down. Select a bright rayon thread which helps define the shape of the crystal.

Stitch about 1/8" from the cut edges of the shape. Either choose a single straight stitch or a double stitch. If you prefer you could also stitch a very small zigzag around the edges for a neater finish.

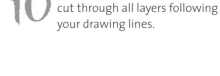

### MAKING TASSELS FOR A FINISHING TOUCH

### BACKING THE PILLOW

**15** Place tassels on top of the pillow with ribbons at corners and tassels pointing toward center. Baste.

See Finishing chapter (page 126) for instructions on backing the pillow.

**13** The tassels are made from zigzagged strips in blues and cream silks.

Each tassel has about 14 strips approximately 10" long.

Lay a bunch of the strips on a flat surface and tie them in the middle with a narrow ribbon.

Fold the strips in half so that the tied ribbon is at the center. Wind a long piece of poly/cotton thread around the strips, half an inch from the fold.

**14** Wrap the area you've twisted the thread around with a braid of your choice (either make it yourself or choose one from your trimmings drawer.

Finally, trim the ends of the strips to the desired length. Repeat to make three more tassels.

**CRYSTAL PILLOW**
*Finished Size 19" x 19"*

Crystal Pillow

# Eternity Quilt

**MATERIALS:**

- 60 ASSORTED RECTANGLES OF SILK 10" x 12" (USE AT LEAST 10 DIFFER- ENT COLORS)

- 30 RECTANGLES OF TRANSFER ADHESIVE 9" x 11"

- VARIEGATED THREAD

- POLY COTTON THREAD

- BATTING 54" x 76"

- BACKING (CAN BE PIECED FROM LEFTOVER SILKS) APPROXIMATELY 51" x 73"

When our son Cameron was 18 months old, David's work took us to the far northeast of Turkey for just over a year. This was a very special time in our lives. Although it was very remote I never felt lonely as the Turks welcomed us with open arms, lots of tea and trays of "Locum" – Turkish delight. It was delightful. David worked very hard but in the time he could take off we travelled through the country and tried to see and experience as much as we could. Through the Anatolian wonderland I made it my mission to collect as many different textiles from the regions we visited. I gathered samples of felt work, rugs and kilims (also fragments of kilims but with beautiful motifs), and embroidered cloth. I found some great examples of color, texture and pattern on the tassels and stitch work on the collars and cuffs of garments, too. These were not just really interesting to look at, but they helped me achieve more of an understanding of who made them, where they were made and for what purpose.

A Turkish friend of mine gave me a book on Anatolian motifs and their meanings and this motivated me to do lots of drawings and design work from them, thinking I'd create something special. Unfortunately I never had the time or the materials while I was there.

When thinking about a project for this book I thought this was the perfect opportunity to design a quilt, inspired by these motifs. The motif of the "Tree of Life" symbolizes ever growing life, beauty and eternity. I discovered that the tree has been used in a stylized way in all kinds of craft work, i.e., stone carving, pottery, wood, glass and woven cloth.

As I mentioned in the introduction to this chapter, using transfer adhesive is a great way to produce something that looks more complicated than it actually is. Fusing it onto the fabric and then folding and cutting the shapes out was lots of fun. These shapes were then fused to the patchwork background of colors reflecting the stone, earth and water. I chose a palette of color and used them both in the background and the foreground which helps to balance the piece visually.

# Eternity Quilt

# Eternity Quilt

### MEASURING AND CUTTING FABRICS

**1** Cut 60 rectangles 10" x 12" in 10 assorted colors of your choice.

Cut 30 rectangles of transfer adhesive 9" x 11" -slightly smaller than the silk panels.

### SELECTING COLORS FOR FUSED SYMBOLS

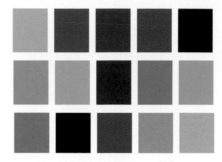

**2** Take three panels of each of the 10 colors and lay them out on a flat surface, 5 panels across and 6 panels down. There should be enough variety of color to have fun deciding where you are going to place them.

### PLANNING THE BACKGROUND

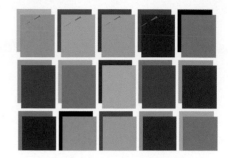

**3** With your patchwork arrangement on the floor, take the remaining 30 rectangles of silk and place them on top of the panels, deciding which color combinations look best to you.

When you have made up your mind, pin each panel on top of its background panel until the cutting and fusing stage.

### FUSING PANELS

**4** Taking each top panel, one at a time, lay the transfer adhesive, paper side up onto background panel and fuse together with a medium hot iron, repeat with the next 29 panels.

### CUTTING OUT MOTIFS

**5** Let your imagination run wild and fold each fused panel either in half or in half again and, draw from the fold, whatever shapes, symbols or motifs you fancy.

I have created 30 different motifs for my quilt but it would look just as good with two or three that you repeated along the patchwork - this is entirely up to you. It can be as complicated or as simple as you desire. (See examples of 10 of the folded drawings I used in the quilt on pages 128 and 129.)

Once you have drawn your design, hold the fabric tightly in your hand and then, with small sharp scissors, cut carefully around your drawn lines.

**6** Unfold and peel the paper off the silk, position on top of its background panel and fuse using a medium hot iron. You can lay a teflon press sheet over your cut motif to protect your iron if you want. Repeat this process with the other 29 cut outs.

### STITCHING MOTIFS TO BACKGROUND PANELS

**7** Use a straight stitch, darning foot with feed dogs down.

With variegated rayon thread, stitch approximately 1/8" from the edge of the motif. A single line of stitching will be enough but of course you can double stitch or zigzag around the shapes too. Do whatever you think looks right for your design.

### JOINING THE RECTANGULAR PANELS

**8** Using the presser foot and feed dogs up, stitch two panels together along the longer sides. Place right sides together and stitch along the edge, taking a half inch seam.

Repeat to make a strip of five rectangles.

Repeat to make five more strips with five rectangles in each strip.

Iron each seam open.

Join strips taking a half inch seam down the long side of each strip, ironing open the seams.

You now should have a panel consisting of five rectangles wide and six rectangles long.

### ATTACHING A BORDER TO THE QUILT

**9** Cut two chocolate brown silk bands, 5" wide by the width of the five panels.

With right sides together, stitch the long length of the bands to the top and the bottom of the quilt. Iron seams open.

Now cut two bands of a purple silk the length of the sides of the quilt x 5" wide. Stitch down both long sides of the bands and iron seams open.

Iron the completed quilt front flat.

### STITCHING BATTING TO THE QUILT FRONT

**10** Cut a poly-cotton batting a few inches larger than the quilt top and pin along each seam line between the 30 panels.

Using a complimentary thread and quilting foot, stitch along all the seam lines both horizontally and vertically ("stitch-in-the-ditch").

### MAKING A DECORATIVE BACKING

**11** Cut five assorted colored bands of silk, and stitch together to create a strip panel the same size as the quilt.

Choose a silk which contrasts with the colors of the backing panel and cut a big rectangle approximately 22" x 30", cut the same size in transfer adhesive.

Fuse the transfer adhesive to the silk rectangle, fold and draw a design of your choice and cut out carefully along your drawn lines.

Open the panel out and peel off paper, fuse the motif in the center of the backing panel and stitch in place along the edges.

To back the quilt see Finishing chapter, page 127.

*Eternity Quilt*

ETERNITY QUILT
*Finished Size 50" x 72"*

# Reversible Orchid Curtain

**MATERIALS:**

- Tangerine dupioni 39" x 78"

- Pink printed chiffon or any silk 39" x 78"

- Transfer adhesive to cover the area 39" x 78" (could be two or more pieces)

- Variegated thread

- Narrow curtain rod

When is a curtain not a curtain? When it's anything you want it to be!

The fronds and the flowers in this piece owe much to my love of the countryside, be it in the forests of Sarawak, listening to the sound of the giant hornbills flying through the jungle canopy or walking through the delicate curling tendrils of ferns amongst the pine trees in the glens of Scotland.

This structure was created by stitching large flowers and fronds through a fused sandwich of chiffon and dupioni. By connecting the stitched shapes together, areas of space between the shapes were created by cutting, making the piece a lacy, intricate free flowing panel.

It's a versatile cloth to hang from the ceiling in front of a window, or behind a sofa as a room divider, suspended as a canopy or simply draped over furniture – or you!

79

# Reversible Orchid Curtain

## PREPARING MATERIALS

1 Cut a piece of tangerine dupioni 39" x 78".

Cut a printed piece of chiffon 39" x 78".

Two pieces of transfer adhesive, both 39" x 39" (two pieces are easier to manage than one big piece).

## FUSING THE LAYERS

2 Find a large flat surface for ironing. Place the first section of transfer adhesive on top of silk, paper side up and iron with medium hot iron. Peel the paper off the silk carefully.

Now lay the pink chiffon edge to edge and on top the silk and place either the paper you've just taken off the transfer adhesive or use a teflon press sheet on top of chiffon. With medium hot iron, fuse two layers together. Before the

next step, flip the remaining unfused chiffon over the top of the area you just fused to keep it out of the way.

Take the second piece of transfer adhesive and place it right next to the fused section you've just done, iron on to the rest of the silk, then peel off paper as before.

Flip the chiffon to lie on top of transfer adhesive and iron this to fuse the two layers together.

Iron the whole panel flat, ironing out any creases.

(This project would work just as well with another dupioni in a contrasting color instead of a chiffon, or perhaps even a tartan or an elaborate printed silk.) Turn the panel tangerine side up and lay it on a flat surface.

## DRAWING THE DESIGN ON THE SILK

3 Start by drawing the flowers in the design (see illustration). Space them out over the length and width of the panel. Draw small and large flowers and change the direction they face.

Once the flowers are drawn, fill in the gaps with curly frond/fern shapes. It is very important to make sure that the lines of your drawing connect together so you are creating interesting shapes between the lines that you will cut out later.

## STITCHING THE DESIGN

**4** Choose a variegated thread and use your darning foot. The thread in the bobbin should also be carefully considered so choose a color which will stand out against the pink chiffon underneath.

Straight stitch either a single line or a double line of stitches around all the flowers.

## CUTTING OUT THE DESIGN

**6** Use small sharp pointed embroidery scissors to cut away all the negative shapes between the flowers and the fronds. Also cut out the three stamen.

Cut a scant 1/8" away from the edges to ensure you don't cut through the stitched lines.

**5** Change the color of the thread for the fronds and switch to a small, open zigzag.

Stitch around the curls and twists following your drawn lines; remember to make sure that your shapes are connecting (see drawing).

Iron the panel flat.

Fold over enough to fit the rod at the top edge of the panel and stitch a straight line across its width, making a neat sleeve to feed a rod through for hanging.

**7** Cut around the fronds at the edges and along the bottom of the panel to give an uneven shaped hemline.

Iron flat.

Insert rod and hang or drape in a special place.

If the large curtain seems like too big a project you could try this technique in a smaller, more manageable version like a scarf.

As in the larger project, use two contrasting fabrics for front and back. The scarf I have made here has a poppy coloured dupioni and slate gray floral chiffon.

Decide what width you want for the scarf and be generous with the length, maybe two yards. Follow instructions for the big curtain and apply to the narrower piece.

The finished scarf could be worn across your shoulders or wrapped around your neck. As you wrap it, twist it around so you see flashes of both sides.

## Reversible Orchid Curtain

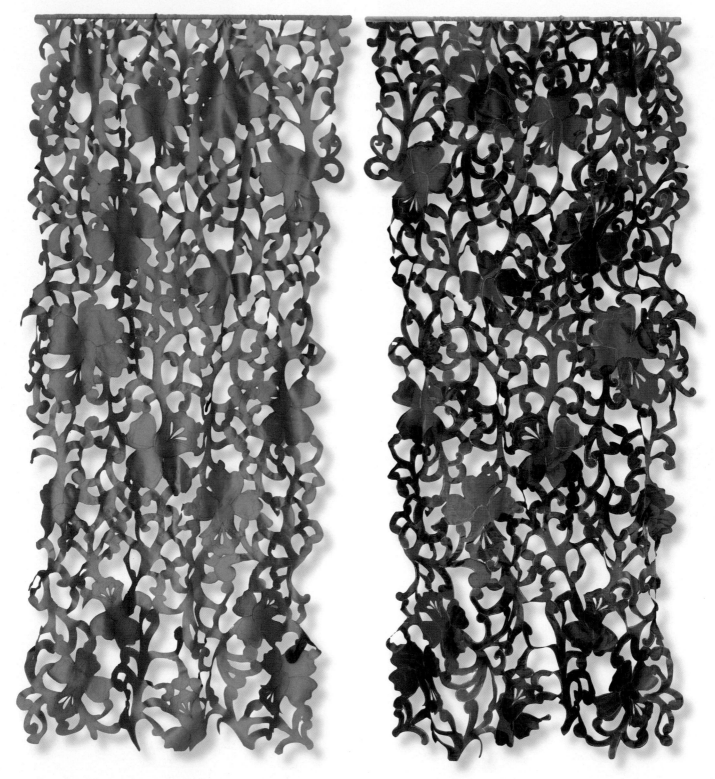

CURTAIN CUT-OUT
*Finished Size 39" x 78"*

# Fused Surfaces and Textures

**D**o try some of these experiments with your bits and pieces around the studio. These surfaces will be useful in the next chapter when they become a layer within a sandwich of silks, making the finished pieces quite unique and exciting.

Gather together a little box of cut threads that have come off your bobbins and top threads, collect slivers of cut silk that you've chopped off the ends of your quilts and considered throwing in the trash thinking you had no other use for them. Keep the warp threads you've gathered together when you've been stripping and ripping silk for the first chapter. Also, fill a box with cut shapes—circles, squares or little strips of different weights and qualities of silk.

Iron transfer adhesive onto a variety of background fabrics, such as chiffons or dupionis in different colors and then either scatter or carefully position the contents of the boxes on the surfaces, fuse them to the background, then stitch. You can stitch in straight lines or grids or try zigzags and big swirling spirals.

I hope you can see the many possibilities with this technique and you're off to raid your trash cans right now.

INSPIRATION

Craft

87

# Nature

# LAYERING

In my second year at the Glasgow School of Art, I remember a very creative still life workshop. Our tutor instructed us to look at the still life in front of us and "draw it" using a bit of glue, handmade painted papers, scissors and our hands. I remember using four or five layers of papers, tissue and tracing paper and then ripping and tearing the shapes of the bottles and plants out of the colorful paper sandwich.

I loved the technique—the interesting torn paper edges, the flashes of handmade paper, the contrasts of colors and textures.

We then took our drawings to the sewing machine and stitched around the shapes we'd made, stitching into the layers defining areas in the composition. Something clicked and I knew that I could do something with this.

I later researched "mola work" which is essentially reverse appliqué using three or more layers of cotton, cut back to reveal the colors underneath. There is a good balance of rich dark colors with brightly colored layers in the designs, something which I also try to achieve in my work.

What really excites me about the layering technique is that you can stitch and cut away to create fabulous, quite intricate patterns but you also create texture, something you want to touch. With the cutting comes the fraying of the edges which, in itself, is another layer and adds something extra to the finished surface. I never turn edges under!

The fusing and layering techniques work so well together and in three of the projects in this chapter I've combined them. In the vest project I've added fused flowers on top of the layers and then cut away the details.

In the kimono and runner projects I've incorporated a fused layer in the sandwich instead of using a store bought print or plaid—so much more interesting, textural and totally unique.

The quilt is an experimental blanket of colored layers and simple cutouts.

Tomoko's pillow is made of scraps a very kind friend sent me from Japan. The simplicity of this piece works for me, the patterned fabrics side by side on a rich dark background with hearts creating rhythm and balance through the design.

I've experimented with sandwiching silks, velvets, plain and printed fabrics together. The beauty of this technique is that anything goes. It's the challenge of gathering the cloth, the colors and the textures together and that's just the start!

# Leafy Bands Quilt

**MATERIALS:**

READ "CREATING THE BACKGROUND"
AND " CUTTING AND POSITIONING
BANDS" SECTIONS FOR ALL THE FAB-
RICS NEEDED FOR THIS PROJECT.

• VARIEGATED THREAD

• BATTING  30" x 58"

• BACKING (CAN BE PIECED)  28½"
  x 55"

Like a lot of my work, this piece was inspired by nature. It has provided us with so many beautiful plants and flowers. In my garden the leaves on the laburnum, hawthorn and oak trees give me great shapes to work with. The mallow, honeysuckle, daffodil, white lily, wild rose and so many more, smell wonderful, look beautiful and constantly feed my imagination and give me fresh inspiration.

Nature abounds with color but nature's palette encompasses a wonderfully subtle range of creams, biscuit shades, buffs and browns. In the quilt I used good accompanying colors like the blues and purples which don't overwhelm the softness of the natural scheme.

When I'm gathering fabric together for the layers in a panel, I try to include a layer using either a fused surface or a patched, banded, collaged surface. When I can create a surface, I can call it my own, I'm not using a store bought fabric but one which is personal and original.

With this panel, the banded background adds more interest to the piece especially when the leaves are cut away. If I'd just used a plain colored silk underneath, it wouldn't have nearly as much character or beauty.

It's so exciting, once the stitching has been done, to take my small scissors and cut away revealing, sometimes, just a flash of an unexpected color.

I've used a variety of leaf and twig shapes here, repeating them along the bands (see my diagrams). This is a simple design which looks more intricate and complicated because of the combinations of colors and shapes. This design would lend itself to smaller products like pillows or bolsters or, on a much larger scale, a bed quilt.

# Leafy Bands Quilt

## CREATING THE BACKGROUND

1 You are creating a stripy, banded background using a variety of different colors that work well together. There are 8 bands in this design, all 30" long but in varying widths.

I have used the following colors:

• Military blue, 11" wide

• Buttercream stripe, 4½" wide

• Navy blue, 6" wide

• Frost blue, 8" wide

• Magenta, 11" wide

• Peacock blue, 8" wide

• Caramel, 6" wide

• Coppery purple, 9" wide

Stitch all these, in order from the top of the list, along their lengths and iron ½" seams open.

## CUTTING AND POSITIONING SECOND LAYER OF BANDS ON TO THE PREPARED BACKGROUND

2 Cut a coppery purple band, 30"x 11" and a caramel silk, 30"x 9½"

Pin coppery purple on top of the military blue band so that you can see a narrow strip of the buttercream band underneath.

Pin the caramel silk centrally over the coppery purple.

Cut a vanilla band 30"x 7" and pin so that 1½" of the navy is showing.

Cut a black band 30"x 9½" and pin leaving an inch of the frost blue showing.

Cut a band of rusty gold band 30"x 8½" and pin centrally on top of the black band.

Cut a band of plaid silk 30"x 7" and pin, leaving an inch of the magenta showing.

Cut a deep purple silk 30"x 6" and pin this centrally on top the plaid fabric.

Cut a thin strip of buttercream striped silk 30"x 1" and pin over the peacock blue band.

Cut a flame yellow band 30"x 10" and pin showing half an inch of the caramel underneath.

Cut a frost blue band 30"x 9" and pin centrally on top of the flame yellow.

Using contrasting rayon threads, blanket stitch the edges along the length of all the bands.

## STITCHING DESIGNS ONTO BANDS OF SILK

3 Working from sketch book designs (see my illustrations), chalk out leaves across the first band with purple and caramel silks.

Use a contrasting thread and straight stitch over the chalked lines. Do a second line of stitches to reinforce this area that you will later cut away.

Working from drawings, repeat this with the next four bands, chalk and stitch.

## CUTTING OUT THE LEAVES

4 To see the layers that I have cut refer to my diagrams.

There is only one of the bands with a single layer to cut through which is the second caramel band, so this one is very straightforward.

With small sharp embroidery scissors, cut away the areas of silk inside the stitched lines to reveal the leaf shapes.

5 On the other four bands there are two layers to cut through. Either refer to my diagrams to see what layers to cut through or decide yourself which color you want to reveal.

BAND 1

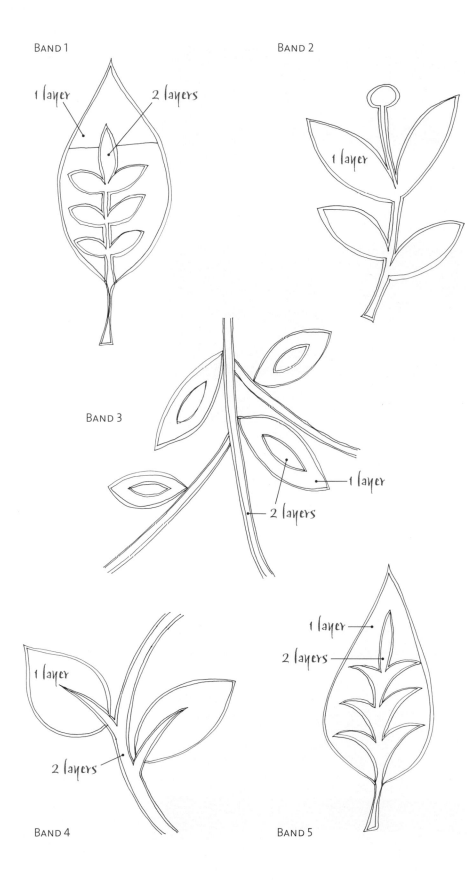

1 layer    2 layers

BAND 2

1 layer

BAND 3

1 layer

2 layers

BAND 4

1 layer

2 layers

BAND 5

1 layer

2 layers

**6** Don't worry if you cut too far down a layer; sometimes the unexpected can work. Even if you accidentally cut through the piece creating a gash in the fabric just use a fused patch of silk on the back and stitch over your lines again.

QUILTING THE PANEL

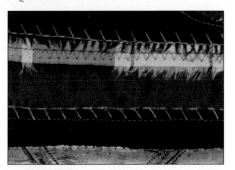

**7** Follow the same steps for quilting as in the Eternity quilt.

See Finishing chapter, page 127.

3 | LAYERING

**Leafy Bands Quilt**
*Finished Size 27½" x 54"*

# Tomoko's Hearts Pillow

**MATERIALS:**

- BLACK DUPIONI 13" SQUARE

- ORANGE/TANGERINE SILK 13" SQUARE

- 16 ASSORTED SILK AND KIMONO FABRICS/SOLID AND PATTERNED/ CUT 49 SQUARES OF 1½"

- TRANSFER ADHESIVE 14" SQUARE

- VARIEGATED THREAD

- BACKING— CUT TWO PIECES 13" SQUARE

- LOTS OF 1" SILK STRIPS TO MAKE TASSELS

n Malaysia I met some lovely ladies who, like me, were there because of their husbands' work. Tomoko and a group of other friends would meet at my house for little sewing sessions when we could. We'd exchange ideas, talk about fabric, cooking, kids, the job, the weather in the UK, Japan, South Africa, Holland, Australia, etc., and sometimes we'd actually do some stitching. We ate a lot, too! Tomoko was great, always very enthusiastic and energetic and would bring fabulous samples she'd worked on from one session to the next.

Anyway, thanks to my pal and the lovely swatches of Japanese kimono fabrics she sent from her home country, I made this pillow. I pulled the fabric from the envelope like a child opening a birthday present, ripping the paper and using my teeth to pull the tape off the bag. I made this in two hours! It's so exciting to have new materials to work with, more so when it's a complete surprise.

Tomoko knows I am a great believer in "Anything goes!" and I chopped up 16 of the patterns and worked them together. It's a simple composition but the colors and patterns do all the work. The heart is a classic motif and by changing the direction of the shape creates movement and visual stimulation.

For a beginner in layering, freehand stitching and cutting, this project would be a good one to start with. Prowl through old boxes of fabric or gather some vintage dresses from the junk shop and have fun chopping.

# Tomoko's Hearts Pillow

### PREPARING THE BACKGROUND FABRIC

**1** Cut a square of black dupioni 13"x 13".

Cut out 49 squares of transfer adhesive 1½" x 1½".

Iron the squares onto a variety of multicolored silks which could be different weights and textures and patterns. I've used an assortment of approximately 16 kimono silks in this piece. Cut around the transfer adhesive to get your prepared squares.

### FUSING SQUARES ONTO BACKGROUND

**2** Arrange 7 squares across and 7 down the black silk leaving a little of the black showing between them and about 1" around the edges. When you are happy with your combinations of colors and patterns, peel off the paper and fuse in place.

### STITCHING THE SQUARES IN POSITION

**3** Cut a 13"x 13" square of tangerine silk and pin this behind the black square.

With contrasting thread and a straight stitch, start from the edge of the black silk and run a line of stitches down the inside edge of all the squares. This creates a fine grid of lines over the surface and holds the colored patches in place. (You could also use a zigzag stitch here instead).

### STITCHING THE HEART SHAPES

**4** Drop the feed dogs and attach the darning foot to the machine. Use a variegated rayon thread to stitch little hearts in the center of each square. Stitch a row of hearts pointing upwards and then a row downwards. Repeat this change in direction across the rows to the end. Iron the piece flat.

### CUTTING THE HEART SHAPES

**5** Use little sharp-tipped embroidery scissors and begin by piercing the cloth through both layers to reveal the orange cloth underneath. Very carefully cut close to the inside edge of your stitched heart. Keep all the tiny cut out hearts.

### ATTACHING THE CUT OUT HEARTS

**6** Pin the cut heart shapes at the corners of all the squares pointing upwards. With the darning foot, stitch a small heart in the center of each heart shape to hold in place.

### MAKING TASSELS & BACKING

These tassels are made from flat strips of silk. See Tufty pillow for instructions, then stitch in place.

See Finishing chapter (page 126) for instructions on backing the pillow.

TOMOKO'S HEARTS PILLOW
*Finished Size: 12" square*

# Chrysanthemum Runner

**MATERIALS:**

- BLACK DUPIONI 17½" x 83"

- TRANSFER ADHESIVE 17½" x 83"

- 1 YARD OF GOLD FOIL METALLIC FABRIC

- 1 YARD OF VANILLA/CREAM PRINTED SILK

- SEE LAYER 2 NEXT PAGE FOR OTHER SILKS NEEDED

- VARIEGATED THREAD

- TAILOR'S CHALK/PENCIL

- SMALL SHARP EMBROIDERY SCISSORS

- BACKING— 17½" x 83" (COULD BE PIECED TO SIZE)

I had such a lot of fun creating the layers in this piece. The first layer is a fused and stitched layer with all my threads and ends off the floor (collected over a few weeks) and the second is a layer made from lovely contrasting bands of silk.

The big chrysanthemums, the third layer, were drawn in a naïve way starting from the center with big petals looping and radiating out from the middle, increasing in size to the edge of the circle.

The rigid horizontal lines where the bands were sewn together have been broken and softened by the swirling, curling shapes of the foliage around the big flowers. The flowers are big but quite subtle when they are cut out and have an almost lace-like quality.

It's very satisfying knowing I've used scraps of silk and the juicy bits out of my trash can to create a sumptuous runner grand enough to dress a baronial table.

When I'd finished this piece it reminded me of some batik I'd seen in Malaysia and Indonesia. Garments made from batik are worn by both men and women and, even in the most rural areas, are the most prominent dress item in their wardrobe. The batiks pictured intricately drawn bouquets and compositions including birds and butterflies or leafy, flowery ornaments.

I'm always on the hunt for inspiration and looking at other fascinating textiles that I find from around the world. They are beautiful and beguiling with the most amazing diversity of styles and techniques.

# Chrysanthemum Runner

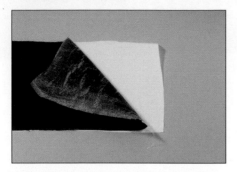

**1** ## LAYER ONE

Cut black dupioni 17½"x 83", cut a piece of transfer adhesive 17½"x 83". Iron transfer adhesive on top of black, keeping top paper attached.

## LAYER TWO:

Assorted colors of silk bands stitched together to make one long panel. Stitch long sides together in the following order:

- Pink silk 17½"x 2½"
- Olive silk 17½"x 3½"
- Kingfisher blue silk 17½"x 14"
- Navy blue 17½"x 5½"
- Buttercream silk 17½"x 31"
- Vermillion silk 17½"x 17½"
- Black 17½"x 5½"
- Cerise silk 17½"x 11"

## LAYER 3

Cut six circles of vanilla and cream print silk and six circles of gold metallic foil fabric all 11½" in diameter.

**2** You are going to cover the long black panel in chopped threads, silks, strips, snippets, anything you can find in your workshop. This is a large area so you will have to gather LOTS. When you have your mound of bits, place them on a large piece of paper and begin slicing through the pile with big dressmaking scissors. Think about the way you chop herbs really finely on a chopping board. You want to keep chopping and slicing through your heap until the bits get smaller and fluffier. You should aim to make fine, confetti-like fluff.

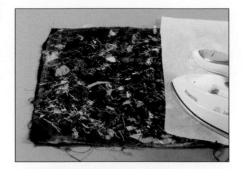

**3** Take your piece of paper with the mound of threads to the ironing board. Take the black fused silk and peel off about 20" of paper, allowing the paper to hang down from the surface. Sprinkle your confetti snippets over this exposed area, dropping it from a height, sprinkling it and spreading it over the surface with your fingertips, trying to cover all the adhesive surface.

Place the paper you peeled off back over the area you've just decorated and iron over it to fuse the bits on to the black.

Peel the paper off to reveal a fabulous decorative, textural surface. Now peel back another 20" of the transfer adhesive paper to reveal another section of black and repeat the sprinkling and scattering of bits as before. Fuse with the iron then work your way to the end of the long panel.

Don't worry if you run out of bits half way through—just gather more, chop and snip to create another pile and continue as before. It adds more interest to the surface if the colors and textures change over the panel.

### STITCHING SNIPPETS IN PLACE

**4** Use a darning foot and a variegated thread or use straight stitch and/or zigzag stitch.

Start at one end of the panel, stitching all over the surface, trapping and stitching down as much of the texture as possible. Look at the back of the fabric to see the stitches you've done and to see whether there are any gaps. Once the length of the panel has been covered in stitches, place the paper you peeled off earlier over the surface and iron the panel flat.

### ASSEMBLING THE LAYERS

**5** Lay the panel of multistriped bands of silk on top of the black fused layer and pin in place around the edges.

Place a cream circle on top of a metallic foil circle and then position all six randomly over the multibanded panel. Pin them in position.

### DRAWING AND STITCHING THE FLOWERS

**6** Using tailor's pencil draw the chrysanthemum design within the circles. Draw the petals from the center out to the edge of the circles.

Using a darning foot, straight stitch over your drawn lines, then stitch again leaving a scant 1/8" between the lines. These lines separate each petal and when cut out creates a lacy, doily-like flower.

### CUTTING OUT PETALS OF FLOWER

**7** Start by snipping around the outside edge of the petals to define the shape of the flower. Cut down carefully through the layer of cream silk to either the organza layer, or the banded panel layer or to the fused layer at the back. It's up to you which layer you wish to expose.

Cut out all the flowers in the runner in this way, choosing different cut layers in each one to make it more interesting.

### DRAWING THE FOLIAGE

**8** Chalk in the shapes of the curly foliage around the big cream chrysanthemums. (See diagram for shapes, page 135).

### STITCHING AND CUTTING THE FOLIAGE

**9** Double stitch around the chalk lines and cut out the areas between the curly shapes revealing the black stitched background fabric. Do this over the surface of the runner. Iron the panel flat.

### STITCHING A BORDER

Cut two 1½" x 83" strips of black silk. Place on the long edge right sides together and stitch. Iron seams open. Cut two strips 1½" x 21." Stitch to short sides and iron seams open.

CHRYSANTHEMUM RUNNER
*Finished Size 78" x 16½"*

# Passion Flower Vest

**M**y stylized passion flower has petals bursting out from its center, like a multicolored firecracker.

With my Mum's help, we took a pattern of a vest I had and redesigned the shape until we got what we wanted. It looked brilliant just with the big fused flowers applied onto the blackberry silk but the best was yet to come.

Using mola, or layering techniques, I achieved depth of surface pattern by following my drawn lines with the sewing machine and binding the five layers together. Trimming away the layers reveals all the colors underneath.

I tried to create a balance of symmetry and asymmetry and contrasting and complimentary colors in the design. The explosion of color on the vest owes much to the natural ability of silk to take dye and reflect light.

The combination of the fused floral shapes and mola, or reverse appliqué technique, is simple to achieve. I've used 3 plain colored silks with a very subtle striped taffeta in the layers along with exotic chiffon fused on top. All in all, a dramatic, rich and sumptuous palette of color. It glows.

Once the layers have been cut away, the areas of the chiffon, left between the layers resembles stained glass, giving the garment an almost medieval look.

## MATERIALS:

- VEST PATTERN
  (SEE PATTERN FOR FABRIC REQUIREMENTS)

- CUT 4 LAYERS OF THE FRONT VEST PANELS IN COMPLIMENTARY COLORS

- 1 YARD OF PRINTED GRAY CHIFFON

- 1 YARD OF TRANSFER ADHESIVE

- VARIEGATED THREAD

- LINING FABRIC AS PER PATTERN REQUIREMENTS

- TAILOR'S CHALK/PENCIL

- SHARP-TIPPED EMBROIDERY SCISSORS

# Passion Flower Vest

## CUTTING THE PATTERN PIECES

## FUSING FLOWERS AND BRANCHES

**1** The vest pattern I have chosen is a long "gilet" style, giving me a large surface area to decorate. I used 4 layers for each of the front panels.

Layer 1 is a striped cream/green taffeta.

Layer 2 is an iridescent green silk.

Layer 3 is an icy blue silk.

Layer 4 is a rich blackberry silk.

Pin all 4 layers together with Layer 1 on the bottom and Layer 4 on the top.

**2** Refer to my diagram for the shape and size of the flowers.

Iron transfer adhesive onto a batik print chiffon. Draw flowers on the paper side and cut out. I've used four passion flowers over both front panels (See drawings for positioning.)

Peel off paper backing from flower and position on the fronts, one flower on the right panel and 3 flowers on the left, then iron to fuse into position. Use a cloth over the chiffon as the glue will stick to the iron.

Use another long narrow piece of transfer adhesive and iron onto a piece of batik chiffon. Draw two long stems with different shaped leaves sprouting out at different angles and fuse this above and below the big flower on the front right panel.

### CHALKING OUT DESIGNS

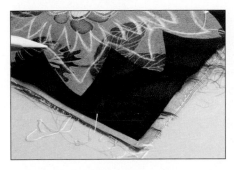

### STITCHING DESIGN ONTO THE VEST

3 Using tailor's chalk, draw the shapes of the flower centers and the petals onto the chiffon and draw vein details on the leaves, and branches.

4 Use darning foot with feed dogs down.

Begin by stitching a wide and close zigzag stitch around the outside edges of the flower in variegated rayon thread.

Straight stitch the flower design by following the chalked lines. Remember to go back over the stitches with a second row to define the shapes of the petals. These lines give the appearance of the lead in a stained glass window when you have cut away the fabric between the lines.

5 Using small sharp scissors, snip out pieces of silk between the lines in the flower to reveal the layers of colored silk beneath.

Cut close to stitching, taking care not to cut the threads (see diagram).

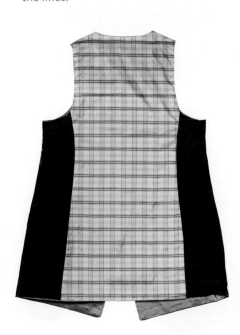

### ALTERNATE COLOR SCHEME

6 When all the flowers have been stitched and cut out, draw and then stitch leaves and branches around the flowers on both panels and cut out as above. See diagram. Stitching lines are red.

Iron both fronts flat.

Attach side and back panels following pattern instructions.

Line and press following pattern instructions.

Wear it and show it off!

PASSION FLOWER VEST

# Ramarama Kimono

**MATERIALS:**

- KIMONO PATTERN
  *SEE PATTERN ENVELOPE FOR FABRIC NEEDED FOR THE KIMONO.*

- CUT ONE COAT IN BLACK AND ONE COAT IN YELLOW SILK.

- TRANSFER ADHESIVE – ENOUGH TO COVER THE BACK PANEL OF THE YELLOW LAYER

- COLLECTION OF STRIPS, SQUARES, SNIPPETS, THREADS—ENOUGH TO COVER THE BONDED SECTION OF THE YELLOW BACK PANEL

- PEACOCK BLUE SILK APROX. 42" x 32"

- TRANSFER ADHESIVE 42" x 32"

- VARIEGATED RAYON THREAD

- TAILOR'S CHALK

- SMALL SHARP EMBROIDERY SCISSORS

- BLACK SILK LINING FOR THE ENTIRE GARMENT/SEE PATTERN ENVELOPE

During our stay in Malaysia we were astounded by the size, the quantity and the variety of insects around us. Throughout the day, we'd see a flash of emerald green from the Raja Brookes Birdwing butterfly, gliding beneath the jungle canopy. After sunset the nocturnal jungle moths were attracted to the lights and in the morning the veranda was a carpet of ephemeral moon moths and a myriad of other exotic bug life.

This mass of dots, spots, scallops, stripes and wavy lines were an inspiration.

The swallowtail butterfly was particularly lovely, with its long tails and scalloped wing markings.

I thought that a surface of feathery strips, silky threads and snippets of silk could capture the irridescence of those minute, overlapping scales on their delicate bodies.

I wanted a large surface area to work on, so I chose a kimono-style coat which is a good simple shape. Again, Mum came to the rescue with a pattern that we could copy.

This project incorporates fusing and layering techniques, creating a unique surface to cut back to. This was a surface that evolved rather than being planned. But I did have to think about the placement of the butterfly (ramarama in Malaysian) shape on the back and what kind of markings would work there. I used paper cut techniques again for the shape of the butterfly, perfect when you want symmetry in the design. The more shapes I cut to represent the markings on the wings meant more interesting contrasts of fabric and texture once the fusing and stitching was completed.

When the butterfly was stitched and cut out, I drew around the shape to emphasize areas around the wings. I particularly like the wave-like

# Ramarama Kimono

shapes on the top wings which stretch past the body of the butterfly and curl and twist over the black silk. Cutting out these areas reveals very subtle threads fading away to yellow silk.

Underneath the butterfly are the architectural/organic shapes which looks like an extension of the butterfly's body. I loved the twisting vines and the antennae shapes around this area which were also the inspiration for the front panels—simple shapes working in contrast with the colourful and elaborate back.

Have fun gathering the scraps, choosing your color scheme and designing your motif for the back. You can't fail to create something wonderful.

1   The kimono is made from four pattern pieces—the back, two fronts and a band around the neck and fronts.

Cut the back and two front panels in a black silk and a yellow silk. Cut the band out of black silk. (If you use a commercial pattern to work with, follow instructions and size guide to fit you.)

## 2 Lay the yellow back panel (T-shaped) flat. Cut the same shape in transfer adhesive.

Fold transfer adhesive in half lengthwise and draw a line from the underarm to the center of the bottom and cut along line. Fuse this to the yellow panel

As in previous projects I created a textural surface of bits. With this project I've carefully considered where I've placed the bits to coordinate with the butterfly design on the top black silk layer (see diagram).

I've used snips of rayon threads on the arms and laid long strips of assorted colors, fanning out from the center back. Underneath the strips I've used assorted strips and snippets, then a section of squares in tones of blues and oranges. For the last section down towards the point, I used horizontal bands of silks, velvets and organza.

However it is entirely up to you as to how you create your surface. You should have developed your own methods after experimenting with the samples in the Fusing chapter. Remember also that not all the surface you've created will be exposed. In places you will cut away little flashes of the background. This is the exciting thing about this technique – there is a surprise element when cutting away an area and a beautiful velvet or a patterned fabric can pop out when you'd forgotten it was there.

Stitch as in previous projects using your darning foot. Change the stitches as you work on the different areas to catch the textures down.

Iron the panel flat.

Pin black silk onto yellow back.

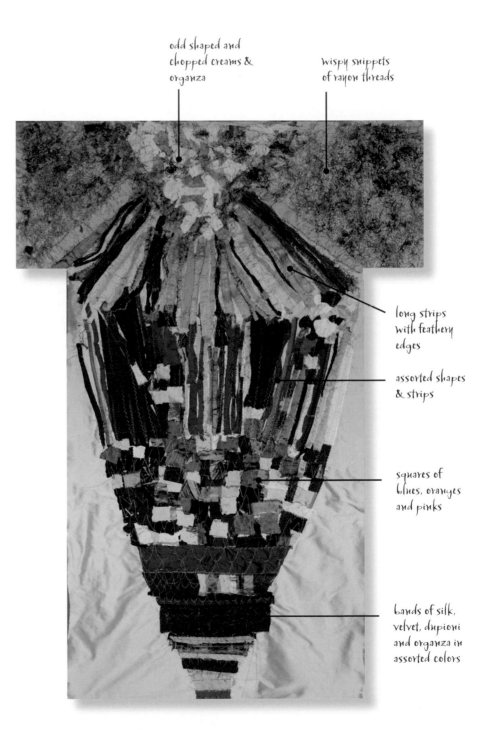

odd shaped and chopped creams & organza

wispy snippets of rayon threads

long strips with feathery edges

assorted shapes & strips

squares of blues, oranges and pinks

bands of silk, velvet, dupioni and organza in assorted colors

*Ramayama Kimono*

### FUSING THE BUTTERFLY

3 Fuse transfer adhesive onto blue silk approximately 25" square.

Fold in half and draw desired butterfly shape onto paper and cut out (see diagram page 136).

Carefully peel paper off and place butterfly with antennae close to the neck edge and lying centrally between the arms.

Fuse with iron.

Repeat with blue silk and transfer adhesive to cut out the hearts and curvy architectural shapes beneath the butterfly (see diagrams). You will need a rectangle of silk and transfer adhesive approximately 10"x 15". For the bud shape at the bottom of the design, cut silk and transfer adhesive 6"x 16". Fold and cut symmetrical shapes.

Fuse in place centrally under the butterfly.

### STITCHING AROUND FUSED SHAPES

4 As in projects before, stitch around every cut edge either with single or double lines. Use a variegated thread contrasting with the blue.

### STITCHING MORE DETAILS

See my diagram – everything drawn in blue are the additional details around the butterfly and stitched into the black silk.

Stitch around twice with variegated thread. To make the markings on the wings more defined, stitch inside the fused shapes on the black silk. When the layer beneath is cut back it gives an almost "stained glass" appearance.

### Cutting through the layers

5 Using small sharp embroidery scissors cut away areas of black silk to reveal textures below and to define the patterns on the wings of the butterfly. Remember to leave a scant 1/8" from the stitch lines when you're cutting.

Cut out the section below the butterfly, snipping away between stitching lines and revealing little flashes of color and texture.

Iron flat.

### Decorating the front panels

6 Pin left black to left yellow and right black to right yellow.

Draw tendrils and hearts (see diagrams page 136). Stitch over chalk lines with double lines in contrasting threads.

Cut black silk to reveal yellow shapes.

### Piecing panels together

8 Follow pattern instructions to sew the kimono together and finish it.

Wear and be happy or hang on a rod, stand back and admire.

7 With straight stitching foot and variegated thread, cover both right and left fronts with vertical lines, stitching over the areas of pattern you've just cut out. This gives the fabric extra body and a rather interesting quilt-like look.

Iron flat.

3 | LAYERING

RAMARAMA KIMONO

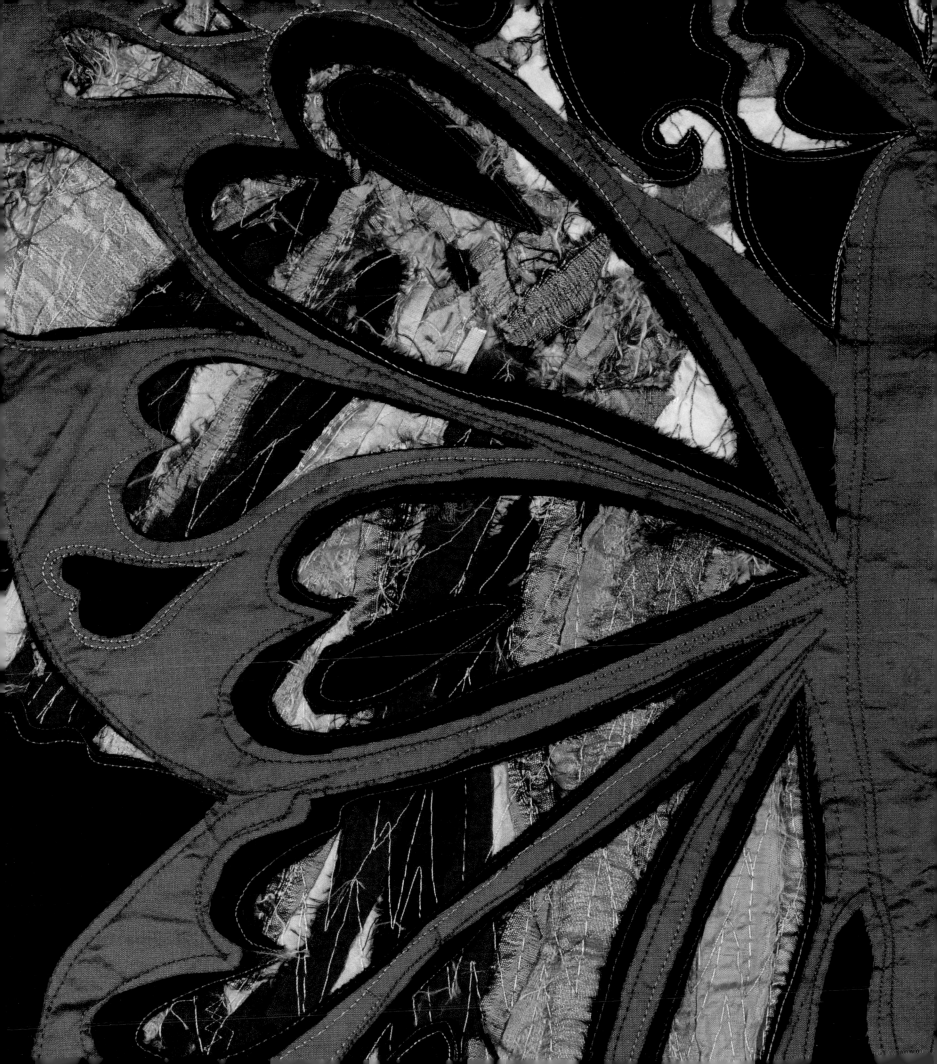

# Landscape

INSPIRATION

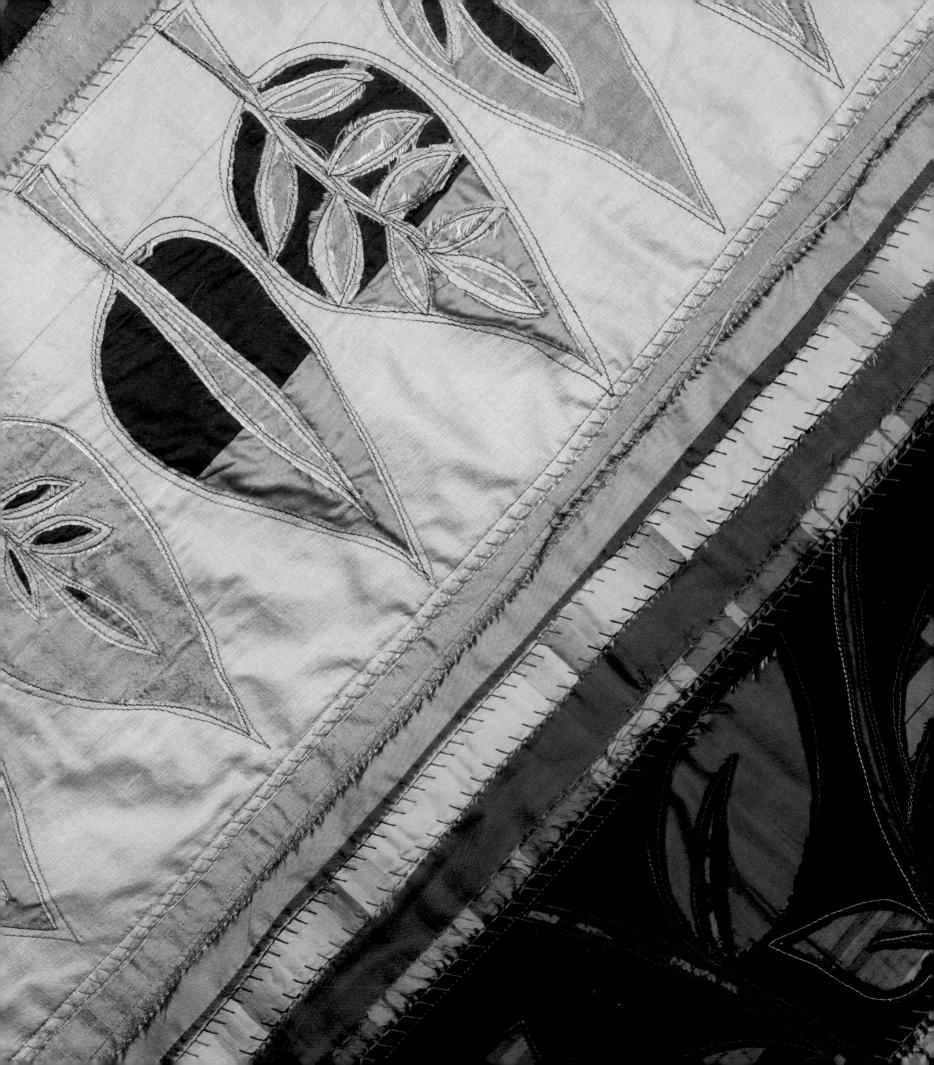

# Finishing & patterns

FINISHING

# Making the backing for a pillow

POSITIONING BACKING PIECES

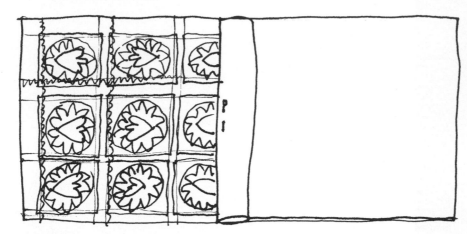

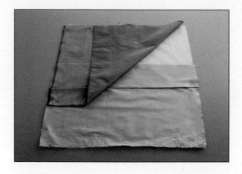

**2** Fold back each overlapping end about 2½" twice, and iron flat. Make sure the overlap is at least 5".

**1** Cut two pieces of silk the size stated in the materials list in contrasting colors.

Place pillow right side up on table.

Place the two back pieces on top of pillow, right sides down. The two pieces should overlap in the center.

**3** At this point you could stitch your name on one of the folded flaps.

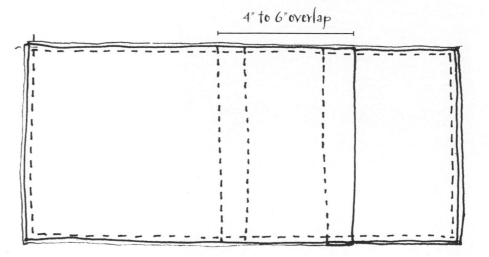

4" to 6" overlap

**4** Pin backing pieces along all four sides of pillow. Stitch ½" around edges.

Remove pins and turn pillow right side out through the central overlapping flap.

Iron and insert a pillow form.

## Backing the table runner

1 The backing could be made by using squares or bands of colored silks to make it unique or to use up scraps.

2 Cut a piece of contrasting silk the same size as the finished piece and pin right sides together on all four sides.

3 Stitch along all sides with a ½" seam allowance leaving a gap of 8" to 12", wide enough to pull the fabric through to the right side when finished.

4 Iron the seams flat and slip stitch the gap closed.

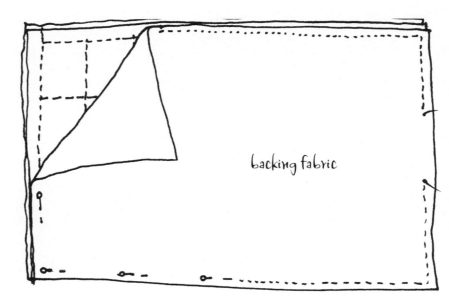

backing fabric

stitch two layers together leaving gap to pull through to right side

## To make a quilt

1 Follow steps 1 and 2 above.

2 Place this piece onto a piece of batting that is slightly larger all around. Pin well on all four sides. See diagram right.

3 Follow steps 3 and 4 above.

4 Then quilt through all the layers using either free-motion or "stitch-in-the-ditch" of the seam lines with regular thread.

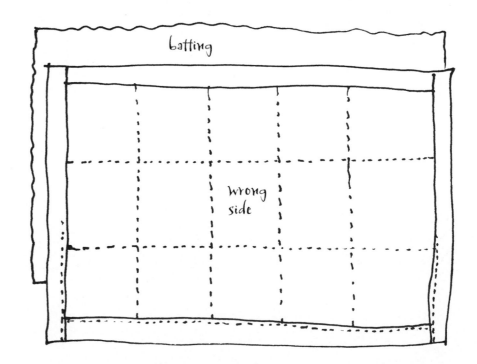

batting

wrong side

# Patterns

## Eternity Quilt

enlarge 200%

fold

fold

fold

fold

enlarge
200%

129

# Patterns

## CRYSTAL PILLOW

fold

fold

enlarge 120%

zig-zag ferns

straight stitch flowers

CUT

CUT

enlarge 235%

# Patterns

## Leafy Bands Quilt

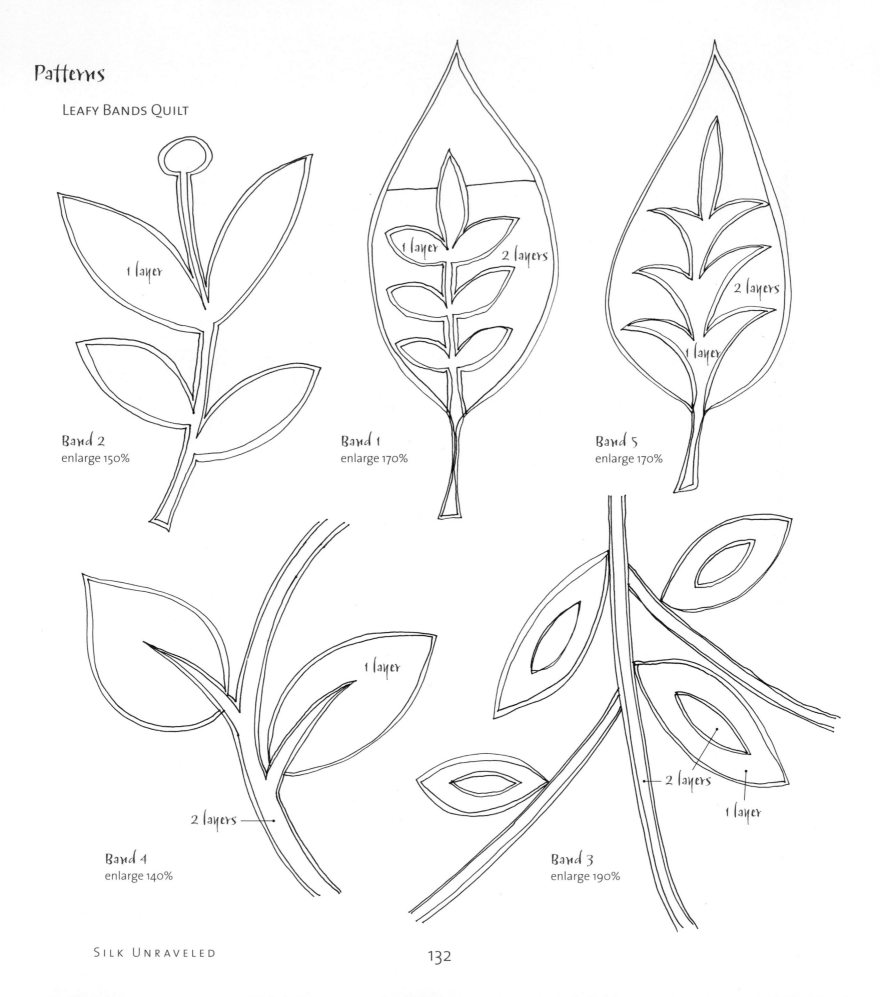

1 layer

**Band 2**
enlarge 150%

1 layer          2 layers

**Band 1**
enlarge 170%

2 layers

1 layer

**Band 5**
enlarge 170%

1 layer

2 layers

**Band 4**
enlarge 140%

2 layers

1 layer

**Band 3**
enlarge 190%

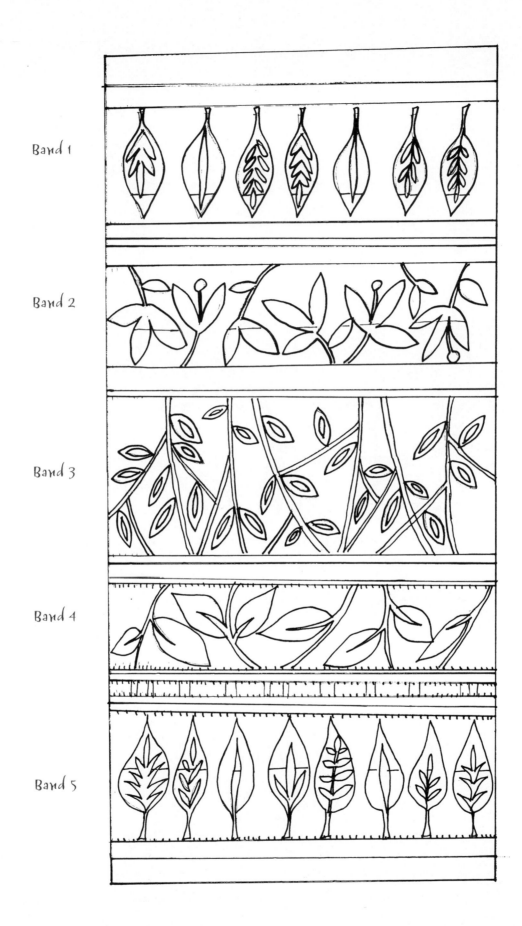

Band 1

Band 2

Band 3

Band 4

Band 5

# Patterns

## PASSION FLOWER VEST

enlarge 165%

# Patterns

## Ramarama Kimono

fold

PATTERNS

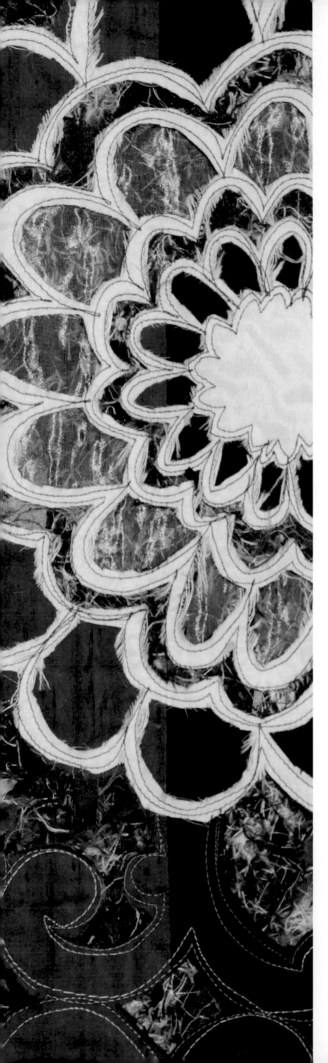

# Resources

**SILK, ORGANZA, PRINTED DUPIONI, CHECKS**

Libas Silks
4400 S. Soto St.
Vernon, CA 90058
800-63-LIBAS
www.libassilk.com

**DUPIONI**

Mandor Textiles
Glasgow, Scotland

Borovicks
London

Broadwick Silks
London

**THREADS**

Silken Strands
UK catalogue

Superior Threads
www.superiorthreads.com

YLI
www.ylicorp.com

**EMBROIDERY SCISSORS, QUILT BATTING**

Cotton Patch
www.cottonpatch.co.uk

**BATTING**

Hobbs Bonded Fibers
www.hobbsbondedfibers.com

**TRANSFER ADHESIVE**

Whaley's
Bradford, UK
www.whaley-bradford.ltd.uk

The Warm Company
for Steam-A-Seam 2
www.warmcompany.com

**CIRCLE ROTARY CUTTER**

Olfa
www.olfa.com

**DRESSMAKING SHEARS**

Gingher
www.gingher.com

Fiskars
www.fiskars.com

**SEWING MACHINES, QUILTING FOOT**

Bernina
3702 Prairie Lake Ct
Aurora, IL 60504
www.berninausa.com

# About the Author

Lorna Moffat is an internationally renowned award wining textile artist, author and lecturer who has been at the forefront of contemporary and innovative textile arts.

After graduating from the Glasgow School of Art in Scotland, her work has been exhibited worldwide in prestigious galleries, craft exhibitions, museums and stores such as Bergdorf's, Barney's, Takashimaya, Nordstrom, etc.

Lorna has also been commissioned for several large embroidered installations for multinational corporate headquarters and healthcare institutions. In addition, she has been instrumental in advancing creative embroidery techniques through her inspirational workshops and lectures together with teaching in schools and colleges around the globe.

Having developed her own unique style in the manipulation, deconstruction and reconstruction of fabrics, Lorna has now taken inspiration from the intricate and ornate craft work of indigenous people in remote corners of the world. Her extensive worldwide travel has also included living within communities in remote mountainous regions of Turkey and in the jungles of Borneo.

Lorna is currently embarking on her next adventure with her husband and two children and is moving from her native Scotland to the wilds of Africa!

Born in Cumbernauld, Glasgow Scotland March 1964

Glasgow School of Art 1982-86 – BA (Honors) Degree in Design

1986-1987 – Postgraduate Diploma in Embroidered and Woven Textile Design

## AWARDS AND GRANTS

Margaret Napier prize for embroidery, 1986

Haldane Travelling Scholarship, 1987

British Crafts Council Equipment Grant, 1990

South East Arts Publicity Grant, 1991

## PUBLIC ART COMMISSIONS

Teachers Whisky Commission, Glasgow, 1988 – textile/wood installation for conference room

Macclesfield Library, 1994—9m x 1.5m wall panel-stitched and printed fabrics

Canning Crescent Mental Health Centre, London, 1995 – Four wall hangings in stitched collage

Quest international perfumers, Kent, England, 1996 – Two panels with words and images in stitch and collage

Medway Hospital, Kent, England, 1997 – a series of three panels for dining room

Brake Brothers (frozen food manufacturers), England, 1998 – 4 large panels in hand-dyed and stitched collage for main headquarters entrance hall and one long panel for the reception area

## Exhibitions Europe

"Glasgow style" in Berlin, 1988

## UK Exhibitions

New Faces, Victoria and Albert Museum, London, 1991

Gifts for Valentines, Victoria and Albert Museum. London, 1992 and 1994

Summer Show, Hitchcock's, Bath, England, 1990 and 1993

Crafts Council Shop, London, 1992

"Out of the Frame", Crafts Council, London, 1992

Glasgow School of Art Textile Group, 1987, 1988 and 1991

"New British Embroidery", touring Great Britain, 1988

Christmas Show, Yew Tree Gallery, Gloucester, England, 1993

The Drew Gallery, Canterbury, England, 1993

"Cushion and Covers", Crafts Council Shop, 1995

Cockpit Studios, London, 1998

Brook Street Pottery, Hay-on-Wye, 1998

"Top Stitch" Exhibition, 1998

Grace Barrand Design Centre, Surrey, England, 1998

Highworth Grammar School, Summer Exhibition, 2000 and 2006

About the Author

## UK Craft Fairs

Chelsea Craft Fair, London, 1989 to 1997

Art in Action, Oxford, England, 1991, 1993 and 1994

Bath Art and Craft Fair, 1991

The Tent, Edinburgh, Scotland, 1989 and 1990

The Direct Design Show, London, 1987 and 1988

"Country Living" Fair, London, 1993

"Ideal Homes" Exhibition, Birmingham, England, 1995

## Trade Fairs

"Creative Eye," London, 1989 to 1992

"International Gift Fair", Jacob Javits Center, New York, 1992 to 2000

San Francisco, Mosconi Center, Trade Fair, 1996-1998

## Textile workshops and Lectures

Beckenham Quilters Guild, 1994

Belfast Embroiderers Guild, 1995

Ashford Quilters Guild, 1996

Glasgow School of Art, 1995 and 1998

Oxford Quilters Guild, 1995

Ashford Textile Group, 1997

Grace Barrand Design Centre Workshop, 1998,1999, 2000

Maidstone Embroiderers Guild, 1998

Embroiderers Guild, Hampton Court Palace, 1999

## Teaching Experience

Crew and Alsager College of Higher Education, on the B.A. textile course, 1987

Cumbria College of Art, 1989

Glasgow School of Art, 1991, 1994 and 1998

Loughborough College of Art, 1992

Ashford Adult Education Centre, sessional tutor for the City and Guild Course, 1990 to 1997

Part time Art Teacher, Highworth Grammar School, Kent, 1995-2001.

## School workshops/residencies

Ashford Independent School for Girls, Artist in Residence, 1992 to 1995

Highworth Girls Grammar School, Kent, permanent artist in residence, 1995-2001

Beavergreen Primary School, Kent – 2 week textile project, 1995

Kennington Primary School, Kent – 4 week project, 1997

Artvin High School, Turkey, project on recycling and craft, 2002

O.S.A., International Primary School, Bintulu, Malaysia, 6 months project for "Golden Tapestry" Commonwealth banner project, 2005

WORK IN MAGAZINES

The World of Embroidery, 1990

Ideal Home, 1990

Homes and Gardens, 1990 and 1994

House and Garden, 1994

Country Living, 1991 and 1993

London Portrait, 1993

Scottish Field, 1998

World of Gardens, 1998

WORK FEATURED IN PUBLICATIONS

"The Art and Craft of Appliqué" by Mitchell Beasley

"Hearts" by Mitchell Beasley

"Decorative Frames" by Collins and Brown

"Cushions and Covers" by New Holland

"Creative Home Crafts" by Dorling Kindersley